AFTER THE
APOSTLES

AFTER THE APOSTLES

MISSIONARY PREACHING OF
THE FIRST THREE CENTURIES

by

JOHN FOSTER, D.D.

*Professor of Ecclesiastical
History in the University
of Glasgow*

SCM PRESS LTD
56 Bloomsbury Street, London WC1

'Αλλά μοι συγγνώμην ἤδη
εὐγνωμόνων ἐντεῦθεν ὁ λόγος αἰτεῖ,
μείζονα ἢ καθ' ἡμετέραν δύναμιν ὁμολογῶν εἶναι,
τὴν ἐπαγγελίαν ἐντελῆ καὶ ἀπαράλειπτον ὑποσχήσειν

My book at the outset claims
the sympathy of indulgent men,
confessing it to be beyond my powers
to undertake the history entire, without omission.

(EUSEBIUS, *Ecclesiastical History* I, 1)

To

KENNETH SCOTT LATOURETTE

who, with regard to the Mission of the Church,

has shown us Church History whole—

ἐντελῆ καὶ ἀπαράλειπτον

First published September 1951

Printed in Great Britain by
Northumberland Press Limited
Gateshead on Tyne

CONTENTS

II.　THE ATTACK UPON POLYTHEISM　47

The use of the Old Testament by Justin is　74
'typological', finding complete forecast concerning Christ, with many forced and fanciful
expositions. Some points are sound enough,
e.g. his claim that Israel's being a light to the　78
Gentiles is fulfilled in the Church. The O.T. is
used chiefly to give scriptural support for Christ;
it was right to desire such support, but it will
be better found as the New Testament documents
become more widely recognized as 'Scripture'.

The use of the New Testament can be illustrated
from the *Epistle to Diognetus* which neglects the
O.T. entirely. To this writer a point of contact　80
with heathen thought is more important. The
Logos was such a point of contact, *cf. Tao* in
Chinese thought. In Justin a 'refrain' of short　83
summaries of the life of Christ points to the
centrality of the N.T.; passages quoted are mostly
Matthew, and the Sermon on the Mount takes
the greatest place. A similar selection seems to
have been made in the first (seventh century)
missionary preaching in China. Irenaeus' words　86
about the preaching's being one and the same,
were true in a still wider sphere.

The life of the Church must be added to its Scriptures as material for preaching if the heathen
are really to hear.

Men preach about their own conversion, as St. Paul
so often did. So Tatian describes his 'deliverance
from 10,000 tyrants' of polytheism; Cyprian,
new birth whereby a man can triumph over sin;
Clement, the joy of youth renewed; Irenaeus, the　89
day when 'God's mercy was upon me'; Tertullian says he was 'born for nothing save
repentance'.

Demonstration of the Christian life is given in one　91
way by Tertullian, the way of biting challenge;

his own missionary work were, a visit to the mother of the Emperor Alexander Severus, and correspondence with the Emperor Philip. He suffered almost martyrdom under the next Emperor, Decius, dying in 254.

PREFACE

WE ARE ALL interested in the Apostolic Succession. Such
interest, however, should not be limited to the Apostles as
transmitters of authority, forgetting the Apostles who were
sent out to preach. They were so sent, before they com-
missioned others. In this central missionary task, who
were their successors, and how did they proceed?

This book attempts to give an answer, so far as answer
can be gained from early Christian literature, especially
from the Apologists of the second and third centuries. The
spread of Christianity is not followed geographically—such
was not the purpose. Rather it was to give contemporary
pictures of evangelists at work, to let the reader 'listen-in'
to bits of missionary preaching, and so to share the experience of early Christianity as an ongoing cause in the pagan
world. Perhaps one of my original contributions may be
keeping in mind throughout, the light thrown upon the
Early Church by situations, as I have known them, in the
Younger Churches. Christian witness in a pagan world is
a subject of which we all have opportunity to know, and in
our own land, nowadays. Here the last chapter may be the
most clearly relevant, if, as I believe is the case, it shows
modern objections by non-Christian intellectuals to be nearly
eighteen centuries old, and to have been answered seventeen centuries ago, by answers which do not fade.

The book is full of paragraphs from early Christian
writers. There are so many as almost to give this volume
value as a source book on the Apologists. All such quotations are in original translation. It is these writings them-

selves, as the footnotes will show, rather than books about them, upon which I have depended. No one, however, could write on this subject without owning a debt to Adolf Harnack.

A German professor told me that his own predecessor in a Church History chair published nothing all his days—'Because,' said he, 'there is no research left to do since Harnack'. It is a sounder tribute than blind following, to say that Harnack's work years ago first kindled my own enthusiasm, turned me to the sources, and left me free to discover for myself. I purposely have not checked with Harnack all the way, lest in the end there should be more of Harnack than of my own findings. I refer to those two volumes of permanent importance, *The Mission and Expansion of Christianity*. The English translation is by James Moffatt, who was later Professor of Church History at Trinity College, Glasgow, and in whose former rooms I write this.

Much of the material in the book was given in lectures at the University College of South Wales, Cardiff, in 1950, and at the University of Oslo, in 1951, and I express gratitude to both Universities for the welcome which they accorded me.

JOHN FOSTER

I

WHO WERE THE MISSIONARIES?

ONE OF THE THINGS WRONG with much of Church History has been that we have left out, for a separate subject called History of Missions, which many seats of learning do not include, and for which, when included, many students fail to find time, that which should be central to the whole, the mission of the Church.

The Synoptic Gospels all reach their climax upon two notes, that of a work completed, and that of a work about to be begun. All that makes for man's salvation has been done. The life and ministry of Jesus, His passion, death upon the cross, and resurrection, leave nothing lacking. And so, 'All authority hath been given unto me in heaven and on earth'.[1] That sounds like the final word. And then, 'Go ye therefore, and make disciples of all the nations . . . and lo, I am with you alway, even unto the end of the world'. The work of witness then begun causes one of the Evangelists, St. Luke, when he has made his 'former treatise . . . concerning all that Jesus began both to do and to teach',[2] to open a second volume, the Acts of the Apostles. What did the Apostles do? Where did they go?

[1] Matthew 28.18f. compare Mark 16.19f. and Luke 24.44-49.
[2] Acts 1.1.

One of the unexpected developments of this second volume is that, having at the outset been reintroduced to that inner circle of the Gospel story, the Twelve, we find them with so small a part to play in the scenes that follow. The commission given them, as retold in Acts 1.8, might well stand as contents page to the book:

> Ye shall be my witnesses both in Jerusalem,
>   and in all Judaea and Samaria,
>   and unto the uttermost part of the earth.

Such are the three sections of the Acts of the Apostles. A glance at the summary set out opposite will show that, in the scheme of writing, the Gentile Mission is that towards which all tends, the Apostle to the Gentiles being the volume's hero. One sign of this is that, already in sections (1) and (2), there are interludes introducing the main figures of section (3).

So far from telling us all that we want to know, the Acts leaves many questions unanswered concerning the Apostles. Although sections (1) and (2) lead up to, and section (3)—more than half the book—centres upon St. Paul, we must still go on to ask how and when and where his missionary journeys ended. St. Peter we have seen at work, among Jews and ' godfearing ' Gentiles, but after he left Jerusalem[3], where was his work continued? St. John, when he has appeared, has been St. Peter's companion. After the mission to Samaria,[4] what did he do? Of the rest of the Twelve, only the early martyrdom of James the Son of Zebedee is recorded.[5] Thus we are left with the surprising situation that the Acts of the Apostles (1) centres upon one outside the original Twelve, yet leaving his story unfinished; (2) completes—in a single sentence—the life of one of the Twelve; (3) gives us a half-told story of another two; (4) and

[3] Acts 12.17.   [4] Acts 8.25.   [5] Acts 12.2.

SECTION	SUBJECT	INTERLUDES introducing section (3)
(1) Witnesses in Jerusalem (chaps. 1-5)	Beginnings: The Twelve, Peter central.	Barnabas (4.36f)
(2) Witnesses in all Judaea and Samaria (chaps. 6-12)	The Opening of the Door to the Gentiles: (a) The Seven, Stephen and Philip central; Stephen's martyrdom, scattering of all except the Twelve throughout Judaea and Samaria. Philip in Samaria preaches to half-breed Jews (Samaritans) and to a 'godfearing' Gentile (the Ethiopian). (b) Peter in Judaea and Samaria; at Lydda, Joppa, Caesarea; At Jerusalem, arrest and escape, leaving James the Lord's brother central.	Saul the persecutor (7.58, 8.1-3) Conversion of Saul (9.1-30) Preaching to pagan Gentiles at Antioch. Barnabas to Antioch, and Saul (11.19-30)
(3) Witnesses to the uttermost part of the earth (chaps. 13-28)	The Gentile Mission: Barnabas and Paul sent out from Antioch. Paul central; his three missionary journeys; arrest, defence and arrival at Rome.	

concerning the remaining nine, tells us, at any rate individually, not one word.[6]

Where may we look for a continued story?

To begin with the Apostle to the Gentiles: In the generation after St. Luke, Clement of Rome (c. 95) seems to have
some additional knowledge. He writes:

> Seven times he was in prison, he was exiled, he was
> stoned, he was a herald both in the East and in the West,
> and won noble fame for his faith. He taught the whole
> world righteousness, came to the limit of the West, bore
> witness before the rulers, and so passed from this world,
> and was received up, into the holy place, becoming the
> greatest pattern of endurance.[7]

Here is an attempt, made early and, made in Rome, to
complete St. Paul's story. It seems to imply release from
his first imprisonment and, a fourth missionary journey, this
time westward, fulfilling his earlier ambition[8] to go on from
Rome to Spain. Still clearer is the implication that his life
ended with martyrdom in Rome. Tertullian (c. 200)[9]
assumes it to be well-known that in Rome St. Paul met the
same death as John the Baptist, i.e. by beheading. Origen
(c. 250) is equally sure that it was under Nero.[10]

To turn now to St. Peter, the first Epistle, which in the
New Testament bears his name, in its opening words sets
him in a missionary relationship to churches in 'Pontus,

[6] Now and again in the narrative they appear collectively, the last time,
apparently, being the Jerusalem Council of Acts 15. It was composed of
'the apostles and the elders', the latter being also called 'the elder
brethren'. How many of the Twelve were there we are not told. When
St. Paul came to Jerusalem after his third missionary journey, Acts 21.17,
he was received by 'the brethren', who are later described as 'James and
all the elders'. The Twelve are not mentioned.

[7] Clement to the Corinthians, 5. He has, in the previous sentence,
mentioned St. Peter as 'having borne witness and gone to the due place
of glory'. In this case there is no mention of 'the rulers' to suggest
that the scene was in Rome; but see below.

[8] Romans 15.24.

[9] On the Prescription of Heretics, 36.

[10] According to Eusebius, Ecclesiastical History, III, 1.

Galatia, Cappadocia, Asia, and Bithynia', and in its final greetings mentions Mark as colleague, and 'Babylon' as the place from which he writes—a name which in the age of persecution, just beginning, was to become an accepted symbol for Rome.[11]   The connection with St. Mark is amplified by Papias, Bishop of Hierapolis (c. 130), who had it from '[John?] the Elder' that 'Mark became the interpreter of Peter', afterwards writing his Gospel from what he remembered of St. Peter's missionary preaching.[12]   In support of the connection with Rome, Ignatius, Bishop of Antioch, gives one hint when he writes to the Romans, (c. 110), 'I do not enjoin you, as Peter and Paul did'.[13] Hippolytus (c. 235) accepts a tradition,[14] known to us earlier only in the Gnostic *Acts of Peter* (c. 200), that St. Peter came to Rome to refute the arch-heretic Simon Magus. Behind this there may be an untainted source from which both writers draw. On the other hand Hippolytus may be beholden to the heretic. Before expressing surprise at such a borrowing, we may well remind ourselves how often still the 'Quo Vadis' legend is used by preachers, not necessarily as historic fact but as pious commentary upon the foreshadowing of St. Peter's death at the end of the Fourth Gospel. The 'Quo Vadis' legend comes from that same Gnostic *Acts*:

> And Peter obeyed the brethren's voice and went forth alone. . . . And as he went forth out of the city, he saw the Lord entering into Rome. And when he saw Him, he said, 'Lord, whither goest Thou?' And the Lord said unto him, 'I go unto Rome to be crucified'. And Peter said unto Him, 'Lord, art Thou being crucified again?' He said unto him, 'Yea, Peter, I am being crucified again'. And Peter came to himself . . . and returned to Rome.[15]

[11] Revelation 14.8, 16.19, 17.5, 18.10.
[12] Eusebius, *Ecclesiastical History*, III, 39.
[13] *Ignatius to the Romans*, 4.
[14] *Refutation of All Heresies*. VI, 15.
[15] M. R. James, *Apocryphal New Testament*, 333.

Eusebius quotes Dionysius, Bishop of Corinth, (*c.* 170), who claims both Peter and Paul as planters and teachers of the Corinthian church, and then adds:

> And in like manner in Italy also, when they had taught in the same place, they bore witness (were martyred) at the same time.

He also quotes the words of a Roman churchman, Caius, of one generation later, with regard to both Apostles:

> And I have the trophies of the Apostles to show. For if you are ready to come out on to the Vatican Fields, or into the Ostian Way, you will find the trophies of those who founded this church.

Eusebius remarks that the names Peter and Paul are preserved in the cemeteries there ' to this day ' (311).[16] And we ourselves may repeat those words, remembering the Church of St. Paul-outside-the-walls (built in 386) upon the Ostian Way, and the Pope's Holy Year announcement of the supposed rediscovery of the tomb of St. Peter, beneath the church which bears his name just to the south of the Vatican.[17] Tertullian (*c.* 200), in the passage already quoted, comparing St. Paul's death with the Baptist's, adds ' Peter endured a passion like his Lord's ', i.e. crucifixion.[18] Origen adds that, by his own request, it was head-downwards.[19] As with the ' Quo Vadis ' story, here again, we may remark upon the good homiletic material, and wonder where history ends and well-intentioned commentary begins.

[16] *Ecclesiastical History*, II, 25.

[17] According to tradition, the body of neither saint has travelled far from the scene of his martyrdom. St. Paul is supposed to have been beheaded on the Ostian Way where now stands the Abbey of the Three Fountains, his remains being placed in the neighbouring Church of St. Paul-outside-the-walls in the fourth century. St. Peter is said to have been crucified within the neighbourhood called ' Vatican ', being buried under the altar of the first Church of St. Peter on the Vatican Hill in the fourth century.

[18] *On the Prescription of Heretics*, 36.

[19] According to Eusebius, *Ecclesiastical History*, III, 1.

With regard to St. John there are fragmentary records of additional events, which it seems best to set down in more or less the order of their supposed occurrence. Tertullian (*c*. 200) says:

> In Rome the Apostle John was first plunged into boiling oil, unharmed; and from there banished to an island.[20]

We have no earlier mention of his visiting Rome, but the island is, of course, Patmos, scene of the Revelation.[21] The Revelation, says Irenaeus, Bishop of Lyons (*c*. 185),

> was seen not so long ago, almost in our own time, towards the end of the reign of Domitian (died 96).[22]

Eusebius explains that, 'according to tradition from the ancients among us', it was in the reaction which followed the death of Domitian that John was able to 'return from banishment and take up residence in Ephesus'.[23] The rest of such information as there is concerns his life there. Irenaeus says that it was in Ephesus that he wrote his Gospel.[24] The *Muratorian Canon* (175-200), without mentioning a place, gives this fuller account:

> When his fellow-disciples and bishops entreated John he said, 'Fast with me now for three days, and let us tell each other whatever may be revealed to us.' That very night it was revealed to Andrew, one of the Apostles, that, with them to refer to, John should make an account in his own name.[25]

Irenaeus has it from the aged Polycarp, Bishop of Smyrna

---

[20] *On the Prescription of Heretics*, 36.
[21] Revelation 1.9.
[22] *Against Heresies*, V, 30.
[23] *Ecclesiastical History*, III, 20.
[24] *Against Heresies*, III, 1.
[25] 'With them to refer to': I have translated thus vaguely, because the Latin word is *recognoscere*, which has three meanings, 'recollect', 'revise', 'authenticate'. Any one of them would fit the context, as describing how the others were to help St. John. We may note that a special association between Andrew and John is already familiar; see John 1.40, Mark 13.3.

(martyred 156), disciple of St. John, that one day in the baths at Ephesus John met Cerinthus the heretic, and came running out saying, 'Let us flee lest the building fall, for Cerinthus, enemy of the truth, is within.'[26] Clement of Alexandria (c. 200) tells a long story, which, he assures us, is not legend but history, of one of St. John's experiences as missionary-bishop in Asia. He was attracted to one young enquirer, and entrusted him as a special charge to the local bishop. Finding on a second visit that the youth had, after baptism, been led astray, and ended as chieftain of a robber band, he called for a horse, rode to the place where the robbers lay in waiting, let himself be captured, and when their chief recognized him and fled, pursued him, and won him to repentance.[27]

Apollonius of Ephesus (c. 197) passes on a tradition that St. John brought some one dead back to life.[28] A late addition (at least we do not find it earlier than this, 388, in writing) is given concerning his old age by Jerome. Each time St. John, too old to preach, was carried into the church at Ephesus, his word of exhortation was, 'Little children, love one another.' When they asked him, 'Teacher, why do you always say the same thing?' he replied, 'Because it is the Lord's commandment, and if this alone were done, it is enough.'[29] Polycrates, Bishop of Ephesus (189), makes the curious statement:

> And there is also John . . . who was made priest, having worn the mitre, both witness and teacher, he fell asleep in Ephesus.[30]

Of his death Irenaeus (c. 185) says:

[26] *Against Heresies*, III, 3.
[27] *Who is the Rich Man who is being Saved?*, 42.
[28] Eusebius, *Ecclesiastical History*, V, 18.
[29] *Commentary on Galatians*, VI, 10.
[30] Eusebius, *Ecclesiastical History*, V, 24. Compare Clement of Rome's parallel between ministries in the Church, and High-priest, priests, and Levites, over against the laity, in the Temple service (I *Clement*, 40-44), and *Didache*, 13, where Prophets are to be given first-fruits, 'for they are your high-priests'.

The church in Ephesus was founded by Paul, and there John lived till the time of Trajan (98-117).[31]

To sum up, whatever the value of some details in the above references, it seems clear that the latter half of a long life did belong to Ephesus. Yet having come to this simple conclusion, we must add the complication of one more quotation, this time from Papias, with Eusebius' commentary upon it. First, the words of Papias, Bishop of Hierapolis (c. 130):

> If anywhere one who had been a follower of the Elders were to come, I used to ask about the sayings of the Elders —what did Andrew say, or what Peter, or what Philip, or what Thomas or James? Or what John, or Matthew, or any other of the Lord's disciples? And the things which Aristion and John the Elder, the Lord's disciples, say. For I used to think that things from the books were not so profitable to me as those from a living and surviving voice.

Eusebius comments:

> It is worth noting that he enumerates the name of John twice. The first of these he couples with Peter and James and Matthew and the rest of the Apostles, obviously meaning the Evangelist. The second John he distinguishes, and ranks him with others outside the number of the Apostles. Clearly he names him 'Elder'. This seems to show the story true of those who have said that there were two connected with Asia of the same name, and that there are two tombs in Ephesus, and that each is called even now the tomb 'of John'. It is well to keep this in mind, for it seems likely, if one should not accept the first, that it was the second who received the Revelation, which book bears in its title the words 'of John'.[32]

The Apostle John, and John the Elder! The chance of

[31] *Against Heresies*, III, 3.   [32] *Ecclesiastical History*, III, 39.

there being two may offer possibilities welcome to New Testament critics. But seeing two people where before there was only one may make a historian ask if this is sober history.[33]

So far we have found additional material only about those who already have the largest share in the New Testament Acts. What of the missing nine? Of these only Philip can claim any mention of comparable significance, and, strangely enough, here again is a case where the careful Eusebius points to two men of the same name and a possible confusion between them. Polycrates, Bishop of Hierapolis (189), writes:

> (Among the saints are) Philip of the Twelve Apostles, who fell asleep in Hierapolis, and two daughters of his, grown old in virginity, and his other daughter who lived in the Holy Spirit, and rests in Ephesus.

Eusebius, after quoting this,[34] reminds us of Acts 21 (8,9) where St. Luke tells of staying at Caesarea with Philip and his 'four daughters, virgins, which did prophesy'—but it is 'Philip the evangelist, one of the Seven'. Can it be that Polycrates means, not the Apostle, but this same Philip, who may have left one daughter at rest in Caesarea, as later he left a second in Ephesus, bringing two, now growing old, to Hierapolis? The only addition then regarding Philip is a blurred one.

Eight of the Twelve remain. Of them Eusebius, who seems to have collected everything he honestly could, mentions only two, referring to a lost work of Origen's (c. 250) as his authority:

> The holy Apostles and disciples of our Saviour, being

[33] I find it hard to take seriously the tradition that St. John was martyred along with his brother St. James. It is mentioned by Philip of Side (c. 430) in what to me looks like a misreading of Papias, and receives no more responsible support. Such a case as can be made for it will be found in R. H. Charles' commentary on Revelation.
[34] *Ecclesiastical History*, III, 31.

spread abroad over the world, Thomas took Parthia, and
Andrew Scythia.[35]

This sounds as though the Twelve in Jerusalem divided the
regions of the world between them. Already in the second
century there was such a tradition, which said that the
division was made, as the election of Matthias had been,
by lot. A book, *The Fortunes* (or Lot) *of the Apostles*, early
put this tradition in writing.[36] In this second century, in
response to men's desire to know more about the greatest
figures of the first, a crop of romances began to appear. It
went on growing in the third century, and far beyond—
stories full of unlikely incidents, and grotesque miracles,
and made the occasion for preaching through apostolic lips
of whatever happened to be the author's favourite doctrine.
If Origen picked out these two, the tradition that St. Thomas
went to Parthia, and St. Andrew to Scythia (i.e. the region
north of the Black Sea), and left the rest, so may we.[37]

The tradition about St. Andrew has made him the patron
saint of Russia. That about St. Thomas has a peculiar

[35] *Ecclesiastical History*, III, 1. He goes on to mention, John, Peter and
Paul.

[36] Mentioned in a list of books to be rejected as apocryphal, the so-
called *Decretals of Gelasius*. Gelasius was Bishop of Rome, 492-6, but
this list may belong to somewhat later.

[37] An excellent article by Dr. R. A. Lipsius in the *Dictionary of
Christian Biography*, ' Acts of the Apostles (Apocryphal) ', is still standard. A list of all the Twelve, with a summary of the supposed mission
of each, and how each died, is translated in Vol. IX of the Ante-Nicene
Christian Library, ii, 130-132. Of the six omitted above, we may note
that:

Bartholomew went ' to the Indians . . . and was crucified in
    Allanum (?) of Greater Armenia ';
Matthew ' fell asleep at Hierees in Parthia ';
James of Alphaeus was stoned by the Jews in Jerusalem, an obvious
    confusion with James the Lord's brother;
Judas ' fell asleep at Beyrut and was buried there ';
Simon the Zealot succeeded James of Jerusalem, a confusion with
    Symeon;
Matthias ' preached in Jerusalem and fell asleep and was buried there
    at the age of 120 years '.

This list used to be ascribed to Hippolytus (c. 235), but is now thought
to be later, and of little historical value.

interest, in that the Syrian Church of South India claims
with one voice St. Thomas as its founder, with confirmation
not only in the apocryphal acts but in our own generation
of critical scholarship. *The Acts of Thomas,* which emerges
probably in Syriac, *c.* 250, in Iraq, begins thus:

> At that season all we the Apostles were in Jerusalem . . .
> (list of the twelve names) . . . and we divided the
> regions of the world that everyone of us should go unto
> the region that fell to him by lot, and unto the nation
> whereunto the Lord sent him. According to lot there-
> fore India fell to Judas Thomas[38] which is also the Twin.

Dr. J. N. Farquhar wrote two essays[39] showing that this
Acts of Thomas has correct knowledge of the route to India,
up the Nile to Andropolis (mentioned by name), then over-
land to the Red Sea; and of an actual reigning prince of
the Punjab about A.D. 50, Gudnaphar, and a neighbouring
prince, Gudi (in the *Acts,* Gundaphorus and Gad).
Origen's connecting St. Thomas with Parthia, Farquhar
suggests, may be because this dynasty was of Parthian
descent. He relates this northern mission to the South
India St. Thomas tradition, by showing that invasions of
the Punjab at this time may have caused an early with-
drawal of the missionaries southward. When I visited
South India and the ' St. Thomas' Christians there,
picturesque survivals of antiquity, I confess I felt almost
ready to share their belief in an apostolic foundation, but
a historian has to have a conscience, and to keep it lively.
The other side of the case has been well put in two later
essays[40] by Dr. A. Mingana. He shows that every mention
of St. Thomas' going to India is traceable to the one source,
this third century *Acts of Thomas,* with no external con-

---

[38] The usual name for St. Thomas in the East.

[39] John Rylands' Bulletins (1926 and 1927), *The Apostle Thomas in
North India*; and *in South India.*

[40] John Rylands' Bulletins (1926 and 1927), *The Early Spread of
Christianity in India*; and *in Central Asia and the Far East.* Dr. Mingana
makes valuable positive contributions also.

firmation whatsoever. For all its internal knowledge of
first-century India, is it sufficient alone?

No one, in quest of the history of the Apostles, can work
through this material, both in the New Testament and
beyond, without being more impressed by the gaps in our
knowledge than by the amount that we do know. It may
well be with some misgivings, and little hope of definite and
detailed knowledge, that we turn to the age after the
Apostles, and enquire, Who were the missionaries?

Christians of the second century were not in doubt that,
with the Apostles, the Lord's commission had begun to be
fulfilled. How could they doubt when with their own
eyes they saw its fulfilment proceeding apace? Justin, from
Rome (c. 150), voices the wonder of it all:

> From Jerusalem there did go out men, twelve in number,
> into the world, and these unlearned and with no ability in
> speech, and in the power of God they proclaimed (Christ)
> to every race of men.[41]

> The Twelve Apostles depend on the power of God, as the
> twelve bells hung on the High-priest's robe, and through
> their voice it is that all the earth has been filled with the
> glory and the grace of God and of His Christ.[42]

In asking who at this time were continuing the mission, we
must first consult Eusebius. He is the earliest (311) church
historian, and to him we have already frequently turned
for all that he collected about the Apostles. In two passages
he goes on to speak of those who were successors to the
Apostles. The first begins:

> And of those who were stars in this period, there was also
> Quadratus. He, tradition says, was distinguished, along
> with the daughters of Philip, for the gift of prophecy. And
> beside these many others were known in those days, who
> held the first rank in the succession from the Apostles.[43]

[41] I Apology, 39.   [42] Dialogue with Trypho, 42.   [43] III, 37.

Notice that the first post-apostolic missionary to be mentioned by name is Quadratus. In the next book of his *History*[44] Eusebius will give Quadratus as the first of the Apologists, presenting a defence of our religion to the Emperor Hadrian (*c.* 125), an apology which is lost to us except for Eusebius' brief quotation. Quadratus was a name common enough, but there are two reasons for thinking that it may be the one man: (1) The first mention of the name is followed by an explanation of who he was. The second assumes that we already know. (2) The first reference speaks of Quadratus as foremost among the successors of the Apostles. The second emphasizes that he 'shows the early date at which he lived' by mentioning that some raised from the dead by the Saviour survived to his own time; and in another place Eusebius calls this Apologist 'hearer of the Apostles'.[45] The point is worth making, as this book has set out to study the presentation of the Gospel to the heathen, as seen in the writings of the Apologists. The chance that the first missionary and the first Apologist are represented by the same name, seems to be a hopeful omen.

Eusebius continues:

And they, as being distinguished disciples of such great men, went on, in every place of the churches, building the foundation which had been laid by the Apostles, further extending the preaching, and sowing the saving seed of the kingdom of heaven widely throughout the whole world. For indeed most of those who were then disciples, soul-struck with a love, more violent than desire for wisdom, towards the divine Word, had fulfilled the

[44] IV, 3.

[45] Against the identity of the two is the usual association of the Apologist with Athens, but this is by no means certain if Jerome was wrong in identifying him with a (later) Bishop of Athens. The mention of Philip's daughters may or may not mean that Quadratus the prophet belonged to Hierapolis. The connection is not a geographic association but fame in the Church's tradition because of a similar gift of inspired preaching.

former exhortation concerning salvation, dividing their
goods among the needy. And then setting out on
journeys abroad, they were fulfilling the work of evangelists, making it their aim to preach Christ to those who
had not yet heard the word of the Faith and to pass on
the scripture of the divine Gospels. And all that these
did was to lay foundations of the Faith in certain foreign
parts. Then they appointed others as pastors, and put in
their hands the nurture of those newly brought in, and
themselves went on to other countries again, and other
nations, God giving them grace and working with them.
For then still a great many wonderful powers of the
divine Spirit were working in and through them, so that
from the first hearing, multitudes together as one man
accepted in their souls reverence towards the Creator of
the universe. It is impossible for us to enumerate by
name all who, from the first succession to the Apostles,
have become pastors or evangelists in the churches
throughout the world. So we have set down suitably by
name in writing the record only of those tradition of
whom, still extant, is borne to us through (their) recollection of the apostolic teaching.

It may sound disrespectful to a great historian, but I cannot
read a passage such as that without being reminded of what
one sometimes finds in a student's examination papers,
when the examiner scrawls at the side, ' Verbiage to conceal
ignorance '. It *is* impossible to give more names, but the
reason is that Eusebius does not know them. Indeed all
that he does know is, somewhat vaguely, that the work
went on.

The second passage is better. It concerns Pantaenus, the
first great figure in a succession of greatness at the theological school at Alexandria. Trained as a Stoic philosopher,
when converted to the Faith, he gave himself not only to
Christian scholarship but to evangelism.

They say that he, in his most ardent disposition, showed

such enthusiasm for the divine Word, that he was even appointed herald of the Gospel of Christ to the nations of the East, and was sent as far as the land of the Indians. For there still were then evangelists of the Word who sought earnestly to use their inspired zeal after the example of the Apostles, for the increase and building up of the divine Word. Pantaenus was one such and went to India, they say. It is reported that, among persons there who knew of Christ, he found Matthew's Gospel to have anticipated his own arrival. For Bartholomew one of the Apostles had preached to them[46] and left with them this scripture of Matthew in Hebrew which they preserved till that time indicated.[47]

In the first passage Quadratus was the one factual figure upon which Eusebius based his vague generalities. So it is with Pantaenus, and again the man we meet is a philosopher. The date must be about 180. As for the place, the word 'India' has been geographically misused (West *Indies,* Red *Indian,* and so on), ever since Columbus made his vast mistake—not only the wrong continent but the wrong hemisphere. The same word had a long history of mistaken identities in the ancient world. Almost anywhere on that journey, when a man was up the Nile, or over to the Red Sea coast, or down to the southern tip of Arabia— before the crossing of the ocean—he might speak of having been to India.

The first picture offered to us, then, is of wandering philosophers, seeking a hearing, endeavouring to make converts. That picture gives a clue which is worth following. What comparable figures do we know in the pagan world, which from what we find about them in pagan literature, might add to our knowledge of the scope for and conditions of such a calling? Cynic or Stoic philosophers had long been known. They took their stand in the market place, urged their gospel upon their hearers—the worthless-

---

[46] See p. 23, footnote 37.   [47] *Ecclesiastical History,* V, 10.

ness of the baubles of this world, the ruin brought by its affections and lusts, and the incomparable value of the soul. The Cynic did it as a popular street-preacher, ready for the give-and-take of repartee, scoring his points with a coarse wit which delighted and augmented his crowd. The Stoic was more polished and prepared. Instead of getting his thrusts home in a free-for-all, he came with a set speech. The 'diatribe' was a style marked by brief periods, carefully balanced, with ascending meaning, making one bit of the subject mean more and more and more. It is often pointed out how this style influenced Christian preaching, notably St. Paul, as when he says:

. . . children of God,
and if children, then heirs,
heirs of God and joint heirs with Christ,
if we suffer with Him, that we may also be glorified with
Him.[48]

Often what the preacher said would be an attack on moral abuses, and the phrases then would not be so much piled up as laid on, each one like the fresh crack of the whip coming down in chastisement. From the crowd they made converts, dealt with enquirers, advised those who came to them perplexed about right conduct, gave the comfort of their religion to those in trouble. These were professional philosophers, obtaining support from their followers and pupils, some of it by regular classes. Epictetus, contemporary with the Apostles, gives advice to a youth who thinks of taking up this profession. He points out that it is not a career but a calling. To go in for it without experiencing the call of God, would be to incur the anger of God and to become a mockery to men. One must be pure in heart, and conscious of being an 'angel' from God to men, in order to speak with that freedom and authority that a preacher needs if he would teach and reclaim.

[48] Rom. 8.17.

Origen himself (*c.* 250) describes these pagan philosophers at work, fully conscious of their similarity to contemporary Christian missionaries:

> Some of the Cynics especially have followed the practice of discoursing in public with those whom they happen to meet. . . . They do not assemble just those who are considered educated, but get a meeting by calling men from the street corners. They do not pick and choose their hearers, but he who wants stands and listens. . . . Those who teach philosophy claim boys for their lectures. They reclaim young delinquents to a better life. They would have the very slaves join in. Yes, boys, slaves, and fools![49]

His point is, if it is right for these to attempt so wide and popular an appeal, why should the heathen objector, Celsus, bring it as an argument against the Christians that they gather a motley crowd?

> We acknowledge that we do desire to educate all men in the religion[50] of God, so as to give boys the exhortation appropriate to them, and to show slaves how to recover freedom of the mind, a mind ennobled by religion.[50] And those among us who are ambassadors of Christianity often declare 'We are debtors to Greeks and barbarians, wise and foolish'.

Origen goes on to claim that Christian preachers are more efficient than the Stoics in the training of enquirers, selection of catechumens, and admission of regular followers:

> Christians, as far as they can, give a preliminary test to the souls of those who wish to become their hearers, and privately give them their first instruction. Then when they think that as hearers—not yet come into the community—they are sufficiently devoted to desire the good

[49] This and the following passages are from *Contra Celsum*, III, 50-54.
[50] Literally 'Word', but he means 'religion' here.

life, then at last they introduce them. They privately form a class for those who are new beginners being introduced, and who have not yet taken the symbol of having been cleansed (baptism); and another class of those who have, as far as they can, themselves made good their choice to desire nothing other than seems right to Christians. Among these certain are appointed to make careful enquiry about the lives and conduct of those who join, so as to prevent those who might commit any infamy from entering their common assembly, while those who are not like this they wholeheartedly welcome and train them to be better with each day.

They are more efficient than Cynics either, for Christians have a Bible-class method which carries men further than mere cross-questioning:

By means of readings and explanations of things read, we lead men on.

Being himself a scholar, Origen is anxious to point out that Christians have not only this popular elementary preaching, but instruction of a deeper kind:

We do everything that we can to secure that our assembly should be made up of wise men, and those things among us which are especially noble and divine we then venture to include in our discourse addressed to the community, when we have an abundance of intelligent hearers, while we conceal and pass by in silence the deeper, when we see that those who gather are simpler folk and in need of such instruction as is figuratively termed milk.

All this seems to put into our picture in a larger way, beyond even what Eusebius hinted, many of those known to Church History as the Apologists. They did not spend their lives writing defences of the Faith. Some of them were men of the kind which Origen here describes, called to, and content with, an insecure, often a hard and frugal life, in order to give themselves to Christian scholarship, and to both popular and scholarly presentation of Christian truth. Such clearly were not only Quadratus whom Eusebius mentions,[51] but Aristides (c. 125) and Athenagoras[52] (c. 177), all said to have been philosophers of Athens.[53] Justin (c. 150), born of heathen parents in Palestine, found his way as a philosopher to Ephesus, and there, by way of the Old Testament prophets, came to Jesus Christ, passing on as a Christian to Rome. Tatian the Assyrian, a philosopher too, met Justin in Rome, where indeed all roads led, and was won by him in a way similar to that of Justin's own pilgrimage. All these after conversion remained philosophers, some, perhaps all, wearing the philosopher's traditional robe. Nor must we forget behind Justin that nameless old man 'of venerable appearance and of humble mien,'[54] who was the means of Justin's conversion in Ephesus. Who was he? Not a recluse, for he told Justin when they met that he was engaged in looking for his family. He too was a philosopher. He used the method of Socratic dialogue, but pointed Justin back to 'certain men more ancient than all who are esteemed philosophers', the Hebrew prophets. These he bade him read, and ended:

> And pray, above all, that the gates of light may be opened to you. For these things cannot be perceived or understood by all, but only by the man to whom God and His Christ have imparted wisdom.

Philosophers too are Pantaenus, who up to c. 190 presided over that earliest centre of Christian learning at Alexandria, and Clement who succeeded him, and, greatest of them all, Origen. So many of the Apologists are really Christian

---

[51] See p. 25.

[52] Of Athenagoras a fifth-century writer says, ' Like the great Paul, from a persecutor he came to be a teacher of the Faith ' (Nicephorus Callistus, quoted in *Dictionary of Christian Biography* I, 204).

[53] But see p. 26, footnote 45.

[54] *Dialogue with Trypho*, 3, 7.

philosophers. Yet we must also remember the more popular side of their work—preachers, evangelists, missionaries.

All this fits well with the glimpse we have from Justin himself of his work in Rome, teaching and preaching, with another Christian's house (Justin lives in his attic) as the address where enquirers can come to be taught more. He gives only a limited picture, because, remember, he is before his judges (163). His own doom is soon to be pronounced, but he does not intend to implicate anyone else.

> 'Where do you assemble?' said Rusticus the prefect. Justin answered, 'Wherever we can. You don't think we all meet in the same place. . . . Our God fills heaven and earth, and is worshipped and glorified by the faithful everywhere.'

(No, no, Justin! You cannot put off the inquisitor so easily.)

> 'Tell me where you assemble. Into what place do you collect your followers?' Justin said, 'I live above one Martin, at the Trinothinian Bath. And during the whole time—and this is the second time I am living in Rome— I am unaware of any other meeting than his. And if any one wished to come to me, I passed on to him the doctrines of the truth.'[55]

Justin tells the address of his own meeting. It will not bring further trouble to Martin, because they already know so much. It was by such knowledge that they had arrested Justin. But he is not going to tell any more, and pretends that he does not know.

Origen gives a picture of mid-third-century conditions:

> Christians do all in their power to spread the faith over the world. Some of them therefore make it their business in life to wander not only from city to city but even to villages and hamlets, to win fresh converts for the Lord.

[55] *The Acts of Justin and his Companions.*

If at the present day, owing to the large number of converts, some rich men of good position and delicate high-
born women give hospitality to the messengers of the
Faith, will anyone dare to assert that some of them preach
the Christian Faith merely for the sake of being
honoured? It is impossible, at any rate reasonably, to
suspect this of Christianity's beginnings, when the danger,
especially to its teachers, was great, while nowadays the
discredit among the majority of mankind outweighs any
supposed honour among fellow-believers.[56]

Origen throughout the *Contra Celsum* is replying to
Celsus who wrote an attack on Christianity in a book called
The True Religion about A.D. 175. It is significant that
among the comparatively few clues to missionary work in
the early centuries, we should find this passage, so sensitive
and alert against criticism. Evidently such charges were by
no means unknown. One who leaves home and wanders
abroad for the Gospel's sake, may easily be labelled fanatic,
or his motives may be sought in some secret gain—an easy
living, a not too hardly won prestige. One is reminded of
anti-missionary sentiment common in our own time among
Europeans in India, the colonies, and the former treaty-
ports of the China coast. Of non-Christian criticism in the
second century Lucian affords another example:

If any imposter or trickster who knows how to manage
things comes among them (the Christians), he soon grows
rich, imposing on these foolish folk.

There follows the detailed story of a rascal called Peregrine,
who after being a Christian missionary, ends up as travelling philosopher—pagan again:

Peregrine left his home country to wander about, and he
had the Christians as a sufficient source of supplies. He
was cared for by them most ungrudgingly.[57]

If non-Christians are laughing about it, *Didache*, a handbook of instructions for churchmen, reflecting, it is thought, conditions in second-century Syria, gives serious warnings to a young Church:

As touching apostles and prophets . . . so do ye.

(We might paraphrase, 'missionaries and preachers'.)

> Let every apostle that comes to you be received as the Lord. And he shall stay one day, and if need be the next also, but if he stays three, he is a false prophet. And when he goes forth, let him take nothing but bread till he reach his lodging, and if he asks for money, he is a false prophet. . . . Not every one that speaks in the spirit is a prophet, only if he has the manners of the Lord. And no prophet that under inspiration orders a table, shall eat of it, or else he is a false prophet. . . . Who ever shall say under inspiration 'Give me money' or any other thing, you shall not listen to him; but if he bid you give to others that are in need, let no man judge him.[58]

Here we see the paradoxical situation in the Early Church. Until the Church is further developed, missionary expansion has to depend on movements of spontaneous enthusiasm, unregulated, without checks upon abuse. Since there is no sending agency to select missionary candidates, here are instructions to the receiving end, on how to judge true missionaries from false. But if the local church is weak enough to need the visiting missionary, how can it be strong enough to sit in judgment upon him?

This situation however may be compared with that of worship. Many in the church set great store upon the excitable preaching and prayers of those called 'prophets'. But there were also those who ruled the church and led its *ordered* worship, and in the developing church it was this element which was to count for most. So with regard to missionary expansion: The evangelist whose authority was simply the call of God in his heart, was not all.

[58] *Didache*, II.

Ignatius, Bishop of Antioch (115), writing to his brother bishop of Smyrna, Polycarp, bids him, 'Press forward in your course and exhort all that they may be saved'. At the end of the third century, *Apostolic Constitutions* says to bishops generally:

> Warn and reprove the uninstructed with boldness, teach the ignorant, confirm those that understand, bring back those that go astray.[59]

Here we have evangelism of those as yet uninstructed, unsaved, set high among a bishop's duties. That means presbyters too, since a bishop shares with presbyters so many of his tasks. Moreover in both centuries we have notable examples of the missionary-bishop. If among those usually called Apologists, we recognized some to be Christian philosophers who did propaganda of this (so to speak) unofficial kind, others we must now recognize as bishops. Among second-century Apologists are Theophilus of Antioch (170), Melito of Sardis and Apollinaris of Hierapolis (175). One of Origen's students, Gregory, called *Thaumatourgos*,[60] became a missionary-bishop (240), and leader of the first extensive mass movement in Christian history, in Pontus. Contemporary with Origen was another great Apologist, Cyprian, Bishop of Carthage. Cyprian himself describes his missionary preaching in the market place at a time of persecution, when he dares the authorities to arrest him (250). If Pantaenus the Philosopher (180) is supposed to have gone to 'India', we know of one whose journey (295) cannot well be anywhere but the real India:

> Dudi (David), Bishop of Basrah, an eminent doctor, left his see and went to India where he converted many people.[61]

[59] *Apostolic Constitutions*, II, 6.
[60] = 'Wonder-worker', see p. 108.
[61] Quoted from Syriac documents by Mingana, *The Early Spread of Christianity in India*, 450; *Chronique de Seert in Patrologie Orientale* iv, 236, 292.

The abuses, considered above, may explain the passing, from the centre of the picture, of the spontaneous enthusiast, and his being superseded by his clerical and authorized counterpart.[62] This is not to say that the spontaneous faded away, for in the third and fourth centuries are the beginnings of monasticism, originally a movement of 'lay' enthusiasm, already in the fifth century the driving force behind new missionary effort (not least those of Celtic monasteries), and to remain so throughout the vast missionary achievement of the medieval Church.

As well as the contribution of those who were full-time missionaries, something should be said of lay evangelism. The section of the World Council of Churches' first Assembly, 1948, dealing with Evangelism, began its report:

This is *the* day of opportunity for the lay membership of the Church.

It went on to point out that it is hard to imagine how Christianity can penetrate certain areas of modern life except through Christian laymen. There is plenty of evidence that one factor in Christianity's first swift spread was laymen, purposefully using the ordinary contacts of life to influence their non-Christian neighbours. The best picture is given by the second-century Celsus, the more welcome since he is engaged as a writer not in idealizing but in vilifying the Church:

We see in private houses, workers in wool and leather, washermen, and persons of the most uneducated and rustic kind. They would not venture to open their mouths in the presence of their elders or their wiser masters. But they get hold of the children privately and

[62] Such a trend can be seen for example in *Apostolic Constitutions*, VIII, from the first three paragraphs of which I quote the following:
' To be a Christian is in our own power; but to be an apostle or bishop, or in any other such office, is not our own, but is at the disposal of God. . . . Nor is everyone who does the work of a prophet holy, nor everyone that casts out devils religious. . . . But now we must hurry along to the main subject, the constitution of ecclesiastical affairs. . . .'

any women who are as ignorant as themselves. Then they pour out wonderful statements: 'You ought not to heed your father, or your teachers. Obey us. They are foolish and stupid, neither know nor can do anything really good, being busied with empty trifles. We alone know how men ought to live. If you children do as we say, you will be happy yourselves and make your home happy also.' While they are speaking, they see one of the school-teachers approaching, or one of the more educated class, or even the father himself. . . . So they whisper, 'With him here we can't explain . . . but if you like, you can come with the women and your play-mates to the women's quarters or the leather-shop or the laundry, that you may get all there is.' With words like these, they win them over.[63]

He means that to be a sinister picture of Christianity like a disease being spread by the less desirable elements of the population, being caught by the children of the family through the slaves. So to-day might an Indian Brahmin speak of the outcaste quarters of a village in South India. Leatherworkers and *dhobies* are despised there too; and there too it is through the despised that movements have begun among caste folk. With Celsus however it is not merely that this is a religion which is alien, or one which gives to the lowly the idea that they count for something before God. Celsus writes so bitterly because Christianity comes into a household to divide it. We are not wrong in claiming with St. Paul that God has 'committed unto us the word of reconciliation'.[64] But often the progress of Christianity in a heathen society seems to set people at enmity rather. I recall a friendship that began during a visit to India in 1938. I was drawn to an Indian minister of about my own age, of similar education, a minister with me of the same Communion. How much we had in common, in spite of our difference of nationality! Afterwards

[63] *Contra Celsum*, III, 55.   [64] II Cor. 5.19.

I met an older missionary, who some twenty years before had been my Indian friend's schoolmaster, the means of his conversion, and I realized that Christianity meant something to my friend that it had never meant to me. A high caste Hindu, he was baptized at eighteen. And to his mother he was thenceforth dead. If he had ever gone back to his village, he would have been indeed dead. He lived all his life a man with no relations.

> Think not that I came to send peace on the earth. I came not to send peace but a sword . . . to set a man at variance against his father, and the daughter against her mother, and the daughter-in-law against her mother-in-law, and a man's foes shall be they of his own household.[65]

Those words were fulfilled in the early Church. To see what it meant when this thing invaded a family, turn to Tertullian of Carthage (197):

> Jealous no longer, the husband divorces the wife who has come to a new chastity. The son, now obedient, is disowned by the erstwhile lenient father. The master, once mild, cannot bear the sight of the slave who has turned trustworthy. . . . Goodness counts less than hatred of the Christians.[66]

Or, of the same place and time, Perpetua. She had not been a Christian long before arrest, being baptized in prison. But then she had not been anything long. She was twenty-two, a year married, with her first baby at her breast. She tells us of her father's coming to her in prison:

> . . . worn out with suspense. He came up to me to make me yield. 'Daughter,' he said, 'have pity on my grey hair. . . . You were always my favourite. . . . Think of your son—if you went he couldn't go on living. . . .'

[65] Matt. 10.34f.   [66] *Apology*, 3.

So spoke my father out of his love for me, kissing my
hands, throwing himself at my feet, and calling me
through his tears not daughter but 'My lady'. . . . He
spoke such words as might move the whole creation.[67]

Perpetua did not recant.

We can understand the bitterness of Celsus. He thought
of Christianity as a rot which was spreading through society,
even to the endangering of civilization itself. The fact, for
us here, is that it did spread, and not least in ways like this.[68]

In this matter of lay evangelism, there should be noted
the special contribution of women. No one can read the
Acts and the Epistles with any care, and not find women
so prominent as to be startling. St. Luke writes of the
Church 'beginning from Jerusalem', and ending when the
Apostle to the Gentiles reaches the world's capital, Rome.
In almost every city and town mentioned in that progress,
women are foremost in the nucleus of first-believers, sometimes the only ones who cared.

1 In Jerusalem the house of the Upper Room, place of
   meeting during the days of the passion, scene of resurrection appearances, continues to be the home of the
   Church. It is probably to be identified with the house
   of 'Mary the mother of John whose surname was
   Mark'.[69]

2 On to Caesarea, seat of Roman government: The pion-
   eer missionary here was Philip the evangelist, 'who
   had four daughters, virgins, which did prophesy'.[70]
   What a household, with four inspired women
   preachers! What a Church with such a centre!

3 South, down the coast to Joppa: Here St. Peter found

[67] The Passion of Perpetua.

[68] Blandina, slave girl of Lyons, who was arrested and faced the beasts in
the year 177, is a reminder that influences travelled downwards (socially)
as well as upwards. She was a recent convert and her mistress, in the same
band of prisoners, is concerned more for the slave girl's faithfulness than
for her own life.

[69] Acts 12.12.
[70] Acts 8.40, 21.8, 9.

the Church to depend upon 'a certain disciple named
Tabitha, a woman full of good works and almsdeeds
which she did '.[71]

4 North to Antioch, greatest metropolis of the Roman
East:[72] There is no direct mention of women among
Church leaders here, but it is from here that the Gentile
mission begins, and women are prominent in almost
all the centres where St. Paul founds his churches. If we
begin from where he crosses to Europe, this is the list:[73]

PHILIPPI: In the dream a *man* of Macedonia was
crying 'Come over and help us'. When St. Paul
got there, he found a place by the riverside where
'devout *women* came together for worship'. One
of them, Lydia, who owned a dyehouse at
Thyatira, was baptized and all her house.

THESSALONICA: 'a great multitude of the devout
Greeks believed and of the chief women not a few.'

BEROEA: 'Many believed; also of the Greek women
of honourable estate.'

ATHENS: a comparative failure, yet 'certain men
clave unto him and believed, among whom was
Dionysius and a woman named Damaris, and
others with them'. Of the two who seemed to be
worth naming one was a woman.

CORINTH: It was here that St. Paul met Prisca, the
only woman whose name habitually precedes that
of her husband. She counted in the Church for
more than he. They seem to have had head-
quarters in Rome, and branches of the business in
Corinth and Ephesus. So Prisca was hostess of
the church not in one city but in three. She was
instructress of Apollos, helping to make a true
missionary of him. She was personal friend of St.
Paul, so close that he called her by the diminutive,
'Priscilla'.

[71] Acts 9.36.   [72] Acts 11.19, 13.1.   [73] Acts 16.12-18.28.

5 To press on to Rome: The Epistle to the Romans ends
with a list of special messages to twenty-six people.
Of the twenty-six, eight are women, and that in a
man's letter in the first century A.D. Such was the
importance of the female element in the Church at the
world's capital.

There is nothing peculiar to the Apostolic Age in this.
Non-Christian and Christian alike soon come to recognize
that the prominence of women is something characteristic
of Christianity. With the pagan such recognition brings a
jibe, with the Christian a boast. Here are two examples,
and while in each case the writer looks back to New Testament times, their emphasis is clearly influenced by knowledge that things like this have gone on happening ever
since. Julian the Apostate (Emperor 361) tries to discredit
the position to which Christianity has come in the Empire
with the Imperial State Church:

For nowhere did Jesus hand on to you instructions as to
this, nor yet Paul, and the reason is because they never
even hoped for you to arrive at such a pinnacle of power.
They used to be glad if they beguiled *maidservants* and
slaves, and through these the womenfolk.[74]

The other is from Origen:

There was such a charm about the words of Jesus that
not only men were willing to follow Him to the wilder-
ness, but *many women also,* not being put off by the
weakness of their sex, nor by the proprieties.[75]

We heard before what second-century Celsus said about
Christian slaves getting at the weaker members of a household. He is not the only one to sneer at our religion as
being for

[74] *Against the Galileans.*   [75] *Contra Celsum*, III, 10.

the silly, the mean, the stupid, *with women* and children.[75a]

It was a cheap sneer. The women were the means whereby Christianity got into Caesar's household, as early as A.D. 95 (when Revelation was being written). The Emperor Domitian's own niece was condemned to banishment, and her husband martyred. That was early in the long, grim struggle. In the year 303 we find the Emperor Diocletian inaugurating its worst, and final, phase by making his own wife and daughter defile their baptismal robes. The early martyr whom we have reason to know best (he left us no less than seven epistles) is Ignatius, Bishop of Antioch. He (*c.* 115) has been arrested and is being marched by a squad of soldiers across Asia Minor towards Rome. There, he knows, he is to face the beasts in the Colosseum, a prisoner condemned. He writes these letters to churches which have sent to greet him on the way—to greet him, not like a malefactor condemned but one marching to victory. In one such letter he sends greetings to the wife of the governor[76] with all her household and her children. The Roman law condemns him, but the wife of the official who represents and administers that law has been won to the Faith.

Tertullian has been already quoted about troubles in a household divided, and first on his list was a pagan married to a Christian wife. This was a crying problem, for the very reason that so often it was the women who were converted first. Tertullian draws a detailed picture of the clash of loyalties in such a household. There is an early morning service—but the husband has made an appointment for them both to be at the Baths at daybreak. A fast is being observed; that same evening he has asked friends to come in to a meal. She has an expedition of charity;

[75a] *Contra Celsum*, III, 44.
[76] *Ignatius to Polycarp*, 8. The place is Smyrna. This is the natural way to translate it. Lightfoot takes it as a proper name, ' the wife of Epitropus '. This is the Greek word for ' governor '.

just then family business most presses. And the suspicion:
He suspects her going to other men's homes, especially as
it is always 'to the poorer cottages'. She shall not desert
his bed to attend nightly meetings, still less for an all-night
vigil. What goes on at the church? He hears they exchange
a kiss. And her embarrassments: A travelling fellow-
Christian arrives, but dare she offer the customary hospitality? On retiring she makes the sign of the cross over her
bed, over her body—and before his eyes. He wakes to
find her out of bed for midnight prayers. He asks, 'Is it
magic you are up to?' The husband, holding over her the
threat of exposure as a Christian, may blackmail anything
out of her, since thus he holds the power of life and death.
She must preside, as his wife, over club meetings and in
taverns, when she ought to be ministering to the saints—
bawdy tavern songs, instead of invocation of Christ. Tertullian ends the long paragraph, 'All things are strange,
all are at enmity, all are condemned'.

Yet having pictured the cost of it in these dark colours,
Tertullian goes on to say of the pagan husband of a Christian wife:

> He has felt mighty works. He has seen experimental
> evidences. He knows her changed for the better. Thus
> even he himself is, by his awe of her, as one who aspires
> to God.[77]

By the time *Apostolic Constitutions* is written (*c.* 300), it is
assumed that the Christian wife will be a major influence
within her home and beyond it:

> You wives, therefore, demonstrate your piety by your
> modesty and meekness to all without the Church, whether
> they be men or women, in order to their conversion and
> improvement in the faith.[78]

[77] Tertullian, *To his Wife*.
[78] *Apostolic Constitutions*, I, 10.

Libanius is of the fourth century, later than our period. His is the last great name in the list of pagan philosophers. One day he exclaimed, 'Heavens! *What women* you Christians have!'[79] Part of the secret of Christianity's triumph did lie there.

As well as purposeful evangelism by ordinary laity, there was also the leaven of Christian example. This subject will be more fully dealt with in Chapter III, in the section on the demonstration of the Christian life.[80] It is a striking fact that at the very time when horrid stories of lust and crime were circulated against the Christians, their own propaganda could with such confidence point to what life was really like, lived out by Christian standards. Here two illustrations will be enough. The first is from Justin (*c.* 150):

> He has urged us by patience and meekness to lead all from shame and the lust of evil. And this we have to show in the case of many that have come in contact with us, who were overcome and changed from violent and tyrannical characters, either from having watched the constancy of their neighbours' lives, or from having observed the wonderful patience of companions of the road under unjust exactions, or from the trial they made of those with whom they were concerned in business.[81]

That this is no idle boast we who belong to Western Christendom have good reason to know. In the year 264 Gothic raiders took prisoners in Asia Minor, and carried them back over the Black Sea as slaves. It must have seemed that the whole purpose of life was over. But this is the testimony of Philostorgius (*c.* 425):

These pious captives, by their intercourse with the bar-

[79] Quoted in *Dictionary of Christian Biography*, article ' John Chrysostom '.
[80] p. 91.
[81] *I Apology* 16.

barians, brought over large numbers to the true faith. Of the number of these captives were the ancestors of Ulfilas himself (first bishop of the Goths, 341).[82]

The importance of this event is far greater than anyone at the time, or the later historian Philostorgius himself, could have guessed. It is the beginning of the conversion of those barbarian tribes, who, in the fifth century, were to destroy the Western Roman Empire. But for the leaven of Christian example, which had made so many of them at least nominal Christians, they might have destroyed the Western Church.

Who were the missionaries? Our answer has been to examine such records as there are concerning men who gave their whole time to this task; and then to note the importance of lay evangelism, the special contribution of women, and the leaven of Christian example. The final item on our list must be the converting power of Christians under persecution.

Those who suffered for Christ's sake came to be called 'confessors', and those who died for Him were called by the Greek word 'martyrs' which means 'witnesses'.[83] The very words are eloquent of the influence of suffering nobly borne. There is no doubt that Tertullian was brought to Christ by this way. More than once he almost owns it.[84] With Justin, as we have seen, there were other influences, but this was one. And perhaps the brevity of his words cannot be improved upon:

> I myself too, when I was delighting in the teachings of Plato, and heard the Christians slandered, and saw them fearless of death and of all things which are counted fearful, I understood. . . .[85]

[82] Philostorgius, *Ecclesiastical History* II, 5.
[83] In the quotations from *I Clement* on p. 16 this is already implied.
[84] *To Scapula* 1, 5; *Apology* 50.
[85] II *Apology* 12.

II

THE ATTACK UPON POLYTHEISM

WE MAY WELL WISH that someone had done for the end of the first century, and for the whole course of the second and third, what St. Luke seems so admirably to accomplish in the Acts of the Apostles. He makes us feel that we are listening in to the first preachers' haranguing of the crowds; to St. Peter's sermon on the Day of Pentecost, to St. Paul by the city gate at Lystra, on the Acropolis at Athens, or in the court-room of Governor Festus at Caesarea. Yet these sermon outlines alone would be scant evidence of the apostolic preaching. It is the Epistles which contain the more abundant data and the more direct. Letters have been well described as conversations of persons who are absent from each other. Those in the New Testament are the talks of a missionary to his converts. Some passages give us not only what he would say if present now, but a recollection of what he did say in the earliest missionary preaching. Surely this is a summary of what his message had been at Thessalonica:

> Ye turned unto God from idols, to serve a living and true
> God, and to wait for His Son from heaven, whom he
> raised from the dead, even Jesus, which delivereth us
> from the wrath to come.[1]

[1] I Thess. 1.9, 10. It is wrong to think of St. Paul's sermon at Athens as a departure from his usual approach. It is almost exactly this. See Acts 17.23-31.

Some passages in the Epistles have close parallels in the Acts, as if to prove that St. Luke did get his record right. In some cases he may have used these Epistles, and written material like them, as his sources. The best example is Acts 26.18 and Col. 1.12-14. In the first the historian is telling how in that court-room at Caesarea St. Paul described his missionary call. In the second St. Paul the missionary is giving thanks for his converts, and he cannot but remember how he converted them:

I send thee unto the Gentiles
    to open their eyes,

that they may turn from *darkness* to *light*,	Who delivered us out of the *power of darkness*
from the *power* of Satan unto God,	and translated us into the kingdom of the Son of His love;
that they may receive *forgiveness of sins*,	in whom we have our redemption the *forgiveness* of our *sins*,
and an *inheritance* among them that are *sanctified*.	made meet to be partakers of the *inheritance* of the *saints* in *light*.

So one might go on, and not with the Epistles only. Papias, *c*. A.D. 130, wrote that Peter ' adapted his instructions to people's needs, without any idea of giving a connected account ' and then Mark, as Peter's interpreter, ' wrote down accurately everything that he remembered '.[2] In our day we have come to take that seriously, and to sift the Gospels themselves, all four of them, for knowledge of the apostolic preaching.

    It is true that St. Luke has almost no successor as a church historian until we reach Eusebius (311). The only notable exception is Hegesippus, who, about 175, wrote *Memoirs of the Acts of the Church,* in five volumes, now, alas, lost to us except for quoted fragments. Eusebius knew it, used

    [2] Eusebius, *Ecclesiastical History*, III, 39.

it, but evidently hardly considered it worth calling a history. He writes about his own *Ecclesiastical History*:

> We are the first to enter upon the subject. We are undertaking to set forth, as it were, on a lonely journey, without a path.

Why was it that for two centuries and a half it occurred to no one to go on recording 'all that Jesus continued both to do and to teach', as St. Luke by implication described his own second volume? A large part of the answer, surely is that inhibiting expectation of the End, which marked these generations. Perhaps it was necessarily so, since it was a period of persecution: 'Amen, come, Lord Jesus!' But this attitude was something which as necessarily reduced interest in a continuing progress, the Church's fulfilment of its mission.[3]

Those fragmentary sermons of the Acts are not our only knowledge of the apostolic preaching. There is all the rest of the apostolic writings. So with the age which follows we have no continuing record of the Acts to turn to, but there is literature.

Of especial value as evidence of how the Gospel continued to be preached to the heathen, is the work of the Apologists. It may be convenient to set out here the principal items of Apologetic literature up to the time of Origen (250). This list is not complete but contains every Apologist to which we shall refer. The dates are approximate, and intended as a rough guide rather than as a final decision. The name 'Apology' given to these writings, sometimes by the author himself, sometimes by later classifiers of Christian literature, shows that they are usually considered as defences of the Faith rather than as missionary presentations of it. There used to be a slogan, 'Don't defend the Gospel, preach it'. That is not only sound advice. It is

[3] In contrast to St. Luke's interest in progress, from Jewish nucleus through Samaritan and 'godfearing' Gentile converts, to the full Gentile Mission, and the development of that mission to the world's capital. See p. 14.

Author	Place	Date	Addressed to
Quadratus	Athens?	125	Emperor Hadrian
Aristides	Athens	125	Emperor Hadrian
Unknown	Rome?	140	*To Diognetus* (an official?)
Justin	Rome	150	Emperor Antoninus Pius, his son, and 'senate and people of Rome' (His *Dialogue with Trypho* is directed to Jews)
Theophilus	Bp. of Antioch	170	*To Autolycus*, a writer
Tatian 'the Assyrian'	Rome	170	*To the Greeks*
Melito	Bp. of Sardis (Asia Minor)	175	Emperor Marcus Aurelius
Apollinaris	Bp. of Hierapolis (Asia Minor)	175	Emperor Marcus Aurelius *To the Greeks* *To the Jews*
Athenagoras	Athens	177	Emperor Marcus Aurelius
Clement	Alexandria	190-200	*To the Greeks*
Tertullian	Carthage	197	'Rulers of the Roman Empire' *To the Nations* *To the Jews* *To Scapula*, Proconsul of Africa (General) *On the Testimony of the Soul*
Minucius Felix	N. Africa	180	(General) *Octavius*
Cyprian	Bp. of Carthage	250	*To Demetrianus*, Proconsul of Africa *To the Jews* (General) *On the Vanity of idols*
Origen	-231 Alexandria 231- Caesarea	250	*Contra Celsum* is his reply to Celsus' *True Religion* (c. 175)

advice which a sound defence cannot but carry out. Some of the Apologies are dedicated to the Emperor, meant to change, or at least to challenge, his attitude, and that of the ruling class. Most are carefully written documents. Some are literary gems. But even those addressed to an individual, clearly have a wider public in mind; those to an Emperor are an appeal to the whole state. And the most literary among them contains, as we shall see, many popular elements. From them we may know how the Gospel was presented to the common people.

Much of the preaching would doubtless be to small groups, often an incidental opportunity which left little chance for preparation. One needed to be always ready. Perhaps it would be a casual group in the market-place gathering round as a conversation or an argument is overheard, and turns into open-air preaching. Or it might be a family where one member is an enquirer, and on visiting him or her one finds, as Peter did in the home of Cornelius (and many a missionary nowadays), the whole company gathered, parents and children and slaves. This might mean a congregation indeed, scores, or even hundreds. Perhaps more often a servant—in the ancient world that means a slave—gives the *entrez,* and the meeting is unofficial and kept secret from the ' family ', though some of them (Celsus, you remember, says domestics get at the women and children)[4] might find out and attend. The generation of peace (210-250) would give more opportunities of preaching in public. And of course all the time there must have been enquirers, individually and in groups, to be dealt with, from exhortation at the beginning, to doctrinal and moral instruction, and preparation for baptism at the end. Already we have seen examples of the Christian propaganda, in the market-place; among the slaves of a household; in church meetings where outsiders attend, enquirers are welcomed, and catechumens are trained; and in the lecture halls of Christian teachers, philosophers of the traditional kind (but

[4] *Contra Celsum*, III, 55.

how different a philosophy!), with both their regular disciples and their occasional hearers.[5]

Here may be added one vivid second-century picture of Christian evangelism. The scene is Alexandria. The narrator tells how he hears that a notable Christian from Palestine is 'staying hereabouts, and he readily gives talks on the (Christian) profession to those who wish'. He continues:

> Then I went with them. And I came, and stood with a crowd which was standing around, and listened to his words.

A crowd, and, evidently, indoors—it sounds as though the preacher is staying as guest at some large house. Indeed all the signs are of a continuance of 'the church which is in the house', so familiar to us throughout the Acts and the Epistles.[6] We have seen it already in the second century, when Justin showed us where the 'meeting' was held in Rome, at Martin's house near the Trinothinian Bath.[7] Note in the passage quoted below, that in this house not only the preacher is staying (he has to flee elsewhere), but there are other Christians gathered, prepared to add their testimony. Also, it is a place known both to interested enquirers and to the supercilious who come to mock, a regular place of meeting. In part of the record not quoted below, the preacher leaves his address with one enquirer who hopes to visit him in Palestine. The address is, he tells him, that of his own home 'and of those you want', i.e. again a house where a congregation gathers. This is how the preaching is described:

> I came to the conclusion that he was speaking the truth, not with dialectic skill, but setting forth in an artless way and without preparation, what he had both heard and

[5] See p. 30ff.
[6] Rom. 16.5, 14, 15, I Cor. 16.15, 19, Col. 4.15, Philem. 2.
[7] See p. 33.

seen. . . . And even from the crowd standing around
he produced many witnesses in support of what he was
saying. But while the crowds welcomed what he was
guilelessly saying, the philosophers, whose motives were
from secular culture, fell to laughing and scoffing at him,
making jokes and pulling to pieces with immoderate
assurance, bringing to bear, like great armaments, their
syllogisms. But he thrust aside their trifling, and was not
for accepting combat with their artful questioning, but
undaunted, did not break off from what he had to say.
'Why is it,' one of them puts the question, 'that the
mosquito, being smallest in size, and having six feet,
should have wings as well, while an elephant, the largest
of beasts, being wingless, of feet has only four?' . . .
'I could make deductions,' said the preacher, 'for your
problems, flippant as they are, if you questioned for love
of truth.'

At this rebuke the hecklers become noisy, and try to shout
him down. They break up the meeting in a riot, from
which the preacher is got away to someone else's lodging
for the night, 'lest someone might lay hands on him'.
That comes from *The Clementine Homilies*,[8] which has
been well described as an historical novel of the second
century. The story is fiction with regard to the apostolic
figures who are made to appear in it. But a novel can
generally be relied upon to have some relation to facts;
often it will reveal real conditions as they have appeared
in the lifetime of the author. This may well be factual as
a picture of second-century missionary preaching.

What did they preach? This chapter bears the title
'The attack upon polytheism', because this seems to be the
subject generally put first. Here is an early fourth-century
statement concerning the order of steps by which one
ascends from the darkness of heathenism to truth and to
God:

[8] *Clementine Homilies*, I, 9, 10.

Since there are many steps by which one mounts to the home of truth, it is not easy for anyone to reach the top. For when lights are dazzling one with the brightness of the truth, if one does not keep a firm foothold, down one rolls to the bottom again. Now the first step is to understand religions which are false, and to cast aside the impious worship of gods made with hands. The second step is to perceive with the mind the fact that God is one, most high, whose power and providence made the world from the beginning, and direct it towards a future. The third step is to know His Servant and Messenger, whom He sent on embassy to earth.[9]

We find a similar order of procedure described by Origen in the Church as he knew it half a century earlier:

In those being newly brought in, we contrive a disregard for idols and for all images, and on top of this we raise their regard, from the serving of creatures instead of God, up to the Creator of all things, and so bring them to a higher plane.

He too puts teaching about Jesus Christ as the final stage, mentioning in this connection both Old Testament and New, with some critical study of documents where sufficient intelligence is shown:

We clearly set forth Him who was foretold, using as materials both the scriptures which prophesied about Him, of which there are many, and those accurate traditions, for those who are able to listen to more intellectual instruction, in the Gospels and the voices of the Apostles.[10]

[9] Lactantius, *On the Anger of God*, 2.
[10] *Contra Celsum*, III, 15. Origen cannot mean that New Testament instruction is limited to those who are more intelligent. The parenthesis must belong to the word ' accurate ', and the meaning be: ' those accurate traditions—*how* accurate we show to those who are able to listen to more intellectual instruction—in the Gospels and the Epistles '. This fits both the context of his argument in the *Contra Celsum*, and what we otherwise know of Origen's practice. See p. 116.

Both these passages are referring to the training of the convert, but there are many signs that in preaching to the heathen, the order was the same. It is so to-day.

If in China to-day, among people not long converted to the Faith, you were to ask, 'What does it mean to be a Christian?'—the first word that would come to almost anybody's lips would be, *Pu pai p'usa,* 'We do not worship idols'. You may feel that this shows insufficient appreciation as to what is the heart of the matter. You may blame those who taught him, for not putting first things first. That is what I determined to do the first time I had the chance to preach to a non-Christian crowd: 'We are Christians,' I said. 'The name comes from Christ.' Then I told them when and where He lived, and how; and what we, His followers, had come to believe about Him, therefore. . . . But I am not sure that any in the crowd continued to follow me as far as the 'therefore'.

A Christo-centric missionary approach may seem to have apostolic precedent in that first sermon of St. Peter's in the Acts:

Jesus of Nazareth, a man approved of God unto you by mighty works and wonders and signs, which God did by Him. . . .[11]

But it is necessary not to overlook how the sermon begins, 'Ye men of Israel, hear these words'. The same emphasis upon Christ continues to mark the preaching to Jews in the post-apostolic age. In Justin's *Dialogue with Trypho,* he first recounts his own experience of conversion, conversion to Christ through reading of the Prophets:

As for me, a fire was straightway kindled in my soul, and there held me fast love for the prophets, and for those men who are friends of Christ.[12]

He continues with this appeal:

If then you have any concern about yourself, if you lay

[11] Acts 2.22.   [12] *Dialogue with Trypho,* 8.

claim to salvation, and believe in God . . . it is for you
to come to know the Christ of God, and when you reach
the end,[13] to be happy.

Not only does he start from Christ. His whole argument
for forty paragraphs is to show why Christians need not
keep the Mosaic Law—because Christ has abrogated it.
When the Jew objects that Christians forsake even monotheism, worshipping 'another God besides the Maker of
all things—one born of a virgin', Justin gets really into
his stride. From the Jew's own scriptures he preaches
Jesus for over eighty paragraphs more: The Old Testament foretells what Jesus did and suffered; it knows already
of more than one Person in the Godhead; the actual historic
Jesus is its fulfilment; not only is there witness to His cross
and resurrection but to the conversion of the Gentiles and
their coming into that true Israel which is His Church. To
the Jew, first, central and last, alike in apostolic and post-
apostolic preaching, the subject is Christ. But the pagan
is in different case.

Hear St. Paul preaching by the city gate at Lystra:

Ye should turn from these vain things unto the living
God, who made the heavens and the earth and the sea
and all that in them is.[14]

Or again on the Acropolis at Athens:

What therefore ye worship in ignorance, this set I forth
unto you: the God that made the world and all things
therein. . . .[15]

How true to that summary of the missionary preaching,
already quoted, in I Thessalonians: 'Ye turned unto God

[13] The word translated 'perfect' in Col. 1.28, etc. Literally 'finished',
having reached the end. It is a word used in the Mystery Cults for
initiation. Justin may here mean arriving at the end (of a catechumen's
instruction) in baptism, or (of the discipline of life) in death.
[14] Acts 14.15.   [15] Acts 17.24.

from idols, to serve a living and true God.' Instead of the many, the One; instead of dead idols, the Living; instead of false religion, the True—this *is* the gospel, before there is even a mention of Christ. Judging from the Apologists, this approach continues to prevail in the post-apostolic age.

Some of the Apologies begin differently, because they are apologies, and have some special defence to make. The *First Apology* of Justin, for example, may at the outset seem to be nearer to my own poor attempt at missionary preaching. He begins with the name *Christianos*. Then he makes a pun on it, *chrestianos,* which does mean ' excellent ' but by no means proves the excellence of the Christian Faith! Forgive him the pun—there follows this noble declaration of Christ:

> For not only among Greeks through Socrates was (poly-theism) put to shame by *logos* (reason), but also among Barbarians by the *Logos* (Word) himself taking form and becoming man, even one called Jesus Christ; and we obey Him. . . .[16]

The beginning with the name ' Christian ', however, is because he is concerned to demand for Christians a just trial, or rather, the more elementary right of a definite charge, instead of the name's being enough for condemnation. And having, in his appeal to the Emperor, made this point by dwelling on what the name really means, he continues—none of them can long keep away from it:

> . . . we obey Him in declaring that (the gods of polythe-ism) are demons, not only crooked, but evil and profane.

The attack upon polytheism develops fast. It takes a form as old as Isaiah,[17] with a style more pungent and an application more direct. For Isaiah the Jew was writing to Jews about their neighbours; Justin a convert from paganism is preaching to idolators themselves:

[16] 5.   [17] Isa. 40.18-46.13.

We need not tell you—you know—what the craftsmen
contrive of their material, carving and cutting and casting and hammering. Often a sordid pot—and they by
their skill change its looks, give it a shape, and call it a
god! That we count not just nonsense, but blasphemy.
. . . The craftsmen who do it are themselves a bad lot.
I need not enumerate—you know well enough, they
have got every vice. The very girls who help them in the
shop they seduce. What madness, that dissolute men
should be said to fashion gods for your worship![18]

From almost any of the Apologists a passage on this subject,
as pointed as this one, might be taken. Let our other
example be from an Apology which, from its high literary
quality, might be thought to stand farthest from popular
preaching, the *Octavius* of Minucius Felix (*c.* 180). The
social setting is not popular but select. Minucius Felix is
a Christian lawyer in Rome, on holiday, since the courts
are closed for the grape-harvest. Octavius is his bosom
friend, who was used once to sharing his whole life.
Happily he has come to share his Faith, and now, when
business and family have separated them for a time, he is
the lawyer-friend's guest for the holiday. Caecilius, the
third of the party, is not yet a Christian; this walk will do
the trick and change him. They set out from Rome for an
excursion to the seaside at Ostia, enjoying the walk down
the Tiber's bank and the prospect of a bathe on Ostia's
glorious beaches—and as they go they talk. Alas for these
genteel delights! An argument on religion flares up, and
Octavius's attack upon polytheism leaves little traces of
gentility:

With what discernment indeed do dumb animals judge
by light of nature concerning your gods! Mice, swallows,
kites, know they have no feelings. They gnaw them,
trample them, sit on them. Unless you drive them off

[18] 9.

they would nest in the god's mouth. Spiders spin over his face, hang their webs from his very head. You wipe and clean and scrape, and those whom you make and protect—you *fear!* It never occurs to you that you ought to know God before you worship Him. . . . That which supports the general madness is the multitude of mad people.[19]

So far from this belonging to its genteel setting, it is exactly what I have heard a Chinese preacher do (I would not have dared to do it myself) before a workaday crowd such as would come in to rest, and to listen for ten or twenty minutes, in the Gospel Hall of a market town. The preacher would describe, in vivid and outspoken language, the helplessness of an idol as a crow sits on its head and befouls it—and the god cannot even wipe its eyes. Yet they pray to that thing to save them from their troubles! I always felt it questionable form to make fun of anybody's religion. In any case it is never for the foreigner to do things like that. In some lands to-day it would cause a riot, whoever did it. The Chinese crowd, however, seemed to like it, and howled with appreciation not with anger. There is no doubt that many in the second century did so too. Roman society was in a position similar to that of great stretches of the East to-day. The old community religions had worn thin. Belief had, for some, worn quite away. 'A wise man,' said Seneca (he was contemporary with Christ), 'will observe these customs of religion as things which the laws require rather than as things which please the gods.'[20] But not all could continue in such cynicism concerning the deepest things. That explains in the first century the number of 'godfearing' Gentiles whom we find as an outer circle around the Jewish synagogue, waiting only for the Christian missionary to come along and detach them by sweeping them into the inner circle

[19] 24.
[20] Quoted by Augustine, *De Civitate Dei*, **VI, 10**.

of the Church. It explains also the prevalence in the second
century of this policy of ruthless attack. There was then
among many hearers, as there is to-day, a widespread feel-
ing after something better, a search for an ethical monotheism.

Just as outspoken is the Christian attack on the immoral
myths, stories which make a man's objects of worship such
characters as he would be far from respecting if they belonged to his neighbours. The Christian preacher shouts to
the crowd that one would keep such from contact with one's
wife and daughters—lustful, deceitful, designing and
drunken. Says Aristides in a triumphant peroration, ' By
your own laws you condemn the gods '[21]—the standard of
conduct which society requires is higher than your thoughts
of heaven! For outspoken preaching upon this theme, we
may turn again to Justin: These myths, he sees, belong to
the origins of polytheism, and, evil as they are, the so-called
gods can be nothing more than evil spirits:

> The truth shall be spoken. In time past low-down
> demons contrived manifestations of themselves. They
> seduced women, and defiled boys, and showed themselves
> as terrors to men, so that those who did not judge of this
> behaviour by *logos* (reason) were thunderstruck. Carried
> away by fear, and not recognizing them for low-down
> demons, they styled them ' gods ' and hailed each demon
> by the name that each had chosen for himself.[22]

Tertullian (*To the Nations,* 13) brings home the folly of
such religion by the brutal statement that it is the custom
to call Juppiter *Optimus,* ' most good ', yet if anything like
law had been operative when he did what the myths tell, he
would have been divided into two sacks, and dumped.

It was more than jibes. Just later than the period we are
considering (up to 300), Lactantius challenges the heathen
to imitate the Christian propaganda if they want to win

---

[21] *Apology of Aristides.*
[22] *I Apology,* 5.

back converts. He thus contributes to our knowledge of that propaganda itself:

> Let them call us together to a meeting, exhort us to take part in worship of the gods, persuade us that the gods are many, by whose mysterious power and providence all is governed. Let them show the origin and beginning of rites and of gods, how they have been handed down to mortals; explain the source, and what the reason may be; set forth what good comes of worship, what punishment threatens its neglect, why gods should seek to be worshipped by men, how human devotion benefits them, if they are in bliss. And let them confirm all this, not just by their own say-so—for the authority of mortal man can count for nought—but by some divine testimonies, as we do.
>
> This is no case for violence or hurt, since religion cannot be forced. It must be conducted by words, more effective than blows in a matter affecting the will. Let them unsheath the keen blade of intellect. If their reasoning is true, let it be published. We are ready to hear if they should teach. Of course we do not believe those who keep mum, no more than we yield to outbursts of rage. Let them imitate us and set forth the reasoned statement of the whole matter. For we do not, as they complain, entice. We lead, we prove, we show. We keep no one against his will, for he is of no use to God who lacks devotion and faith. Yet no one deserts our side, since truth itself holds him. Let them teach in this manner. . . . But if they did, our 'old women', whom they despise, and 'local boys', would laugh their error and stupidity to scorn.[23]

'We teach, we prove, *we show*.' The 'divine testimonies' to which Lactantius refers doubtless include the Scriptures which will be one subject dealt with in the next chapter. But among the things they 'showed' was the disturbing phenomenon of exorcism. It needs an addendum here.

[23] *Divine Institutes*, V, 20 (abbreviated).

The earliest record of apostolic preaching concerns the send-ing out of the Twelve two by two: 'And they went out and preached that men should repent, and they cast out devils.'[24] The record of the only consecutive missionary work done by St. Paul, the two years' stay at Ephesus, begins with his 'reasoning daily in the school of Tyrannus' and links this closely with the 'special miracles God wrought by the hands of Paul'. It was not only by his hands—a handkerchief or an apron which had been near him was carried away, and 'the diseases departed . . . and the evil spirits went out'.[25] The record ends, 'So mightily grew the word of the Lord and prevailed'. Similar cures, including those 'vexed with unclean spirits' had earlier been seen through Peter in Jerusalem,[26] and after the leaders in Jerusalem were dispersed, through Philip in Samaria, to whom

> the multitudes gave heed with one accord . . . when they heard, and saw the signs which he did, for from many of them which had unclean spirits, they came out crying with a loud voice.[27]

All the way, the implication is that the apostolic preaching won men's attention, and in some cases the response of faith, because the word was confirmed by 'the signs that followed'.[28] And this seems to be prominent, if not chief, among the signs, exorcism.

The writer of the article 'Exorcism' in the *Dictionary of the Apostolic Church* makes this statement:

> When we pass to the literature of the Fathers, we cannot help being struck with the almost total absence of refer-ences to exorcism.

That remark is more revealing of prejudice than of Patristic knowledge. A story was current in Scotland, before the 1929 union of Churches, when evangelical Presbyterianism

[24] Mark 6.12, 13.   [26] Acts 5.16.   [28] Mark 16.20.
[25] Acts 19.12.   [27] Acts 8.6, 7.

was mainly represented by the United Free Church, affectionately spoken of as 'the U.F.'. A small Scottish boy went south to stay with an aunt-by-marriage who was English and Anglican. On the first night of his stay, she tucked him in and said, 'You won't be lonely or afraid. There are angels round your bed.' And a small voice from between the pillows and the eiderdown was heard, 'We don't make much of angels in the U.F.' The writer of that article might similarly excuse himself with regard to devils. Most of us nowadays feel uncomfortable about these phenomena. The scope of the Acts is not wide enough for us to avoid that which is spooky, but in the abundance of later literature we can neglect those bits we do not like. All the same, it must be hard to shut one's eyes to all that concerns the continuance of this apostolic tradition. The view of the Church at the close of the third century clearly is that this is one of the 'gifts of the Spirit' (*charismata*), which has never been withheld:

These gifts were first bestowed on us, the Apostles, as we were about to preach the Gospel to every creature, and afterwards they were necessarily provided to those who through us had believed, not for self-advantage to those energized, but as deposition for the unbelievers, that those whom the word did not persuade, the power of the signs might dazzle.[29]

Notice again the emphasis on the missionary value of these cures.

That quotation was from the so-called *Apostolic Constitutions*. Irenaeus, whose writings are nearer to being 'apostolic' since he was the disciple of Polycarp who was the disciple of John, just takes this miracle for granted as being constantly performed, adding that he knows personally instances even of raising the dead:

It has often been done in the brotherhood, in cases of

[29] *Apostolic Constitutions*, VIII, 1.

dire need, the whole of the local church beseeching, with much fasting and many supplications. The spirit of him who was departed has returned. The man has been granted to the prayers of the saints.

He mentions it again, this time along with exorcism, emphasizing the difference between Christian practice and the magical pretensions of the Gnostics, with regard to methods used:

Some do, really and truly, cast out demons, so that those very ones who have been cleansed from evil spirits often believe, and are in the church. . . . What is more, as I said, even the dead have been raised and remained with us for considerable years. What more? It is impossible to mention the number of gifts (*charismata*) which throughout the whole world the Church has received from God in the name of Jesus Christ who was crucified under Pontius Pilate. . . . Nor does the Church do anything by angelic invocations, nor incantations, nor other perverse meddling. It directs prayers in a manner clean, pure, and open, to the Lord who made all things, and calls upon the name of our Lord Jesus Christ.[30]

This is confirmed by Justin (*c*. 150) who writes about frequent cases everywhere, not least in Rome:

And now you may learn from what goes on under your own eyes. For many devil-possessed all over the world, and in your own city, many of our men, the Christians have exorcised in the name of Jesus Christ, who was crucified under Pontius Pilate. When all other exorcists and sayers of charms and sellers of drugs failed, they have healed them, and still do heal, sapping the power of the demons who hold men, and driving them out.[31]

Notice again the means. To drive out a devil they do not merely recite the Name. They recite the Faith, the Rule of Faith, or, as we should say, the Creed. This is at once the

[30] *Against Heresies* II, 31, 32.   [31] *II Apology*, 6.

ground of confidence for the one who performs the cure, and the way by which he makes the cure itself a proclamation of the Gospel. It is worth noting that if one joins what Irenaeus says (above) about God the maker of all things, with what Justin here adds (below) concerning Jesus Christ, the creed is nearly all there. Clearly it was used to cast out devils long before it was used to excommunicate heretics:

> In the name of this same Son of God, firstborn of every creature, who was born of a virgin, and became man subject to suffering,[32] and was crucified under Pontius Pilate . . . and died, and rose again from the dead, and ascended into heaven, every demon exorcised is conquered and subdued.[33]

Origen (c. 250) adds his testimony. He too mentions the words of the Creed as used in exorcism:

> Some there are who show signs of having received through this Faith something the more incredible. I mean by the cures which they perform, calling upon nought else, over those who need their healing, than the God who is over all and the name of Jesus, along with the account concerning Him. For by these means we ourselves have seen many set free from grievous symptoms and distractions and madness, and ten thousand things beside, which neither men nor demons had cured.[34]

> The Christian, the true Christian I mean . . . will suffer nothing from demons, for lo, he is mightier than demons.[35]

> Not a few Christians exorcise sufferers, and that without manipulations and magic or the use of drugs, but just by prayer and an invocation of the simpler kind, and such means as the simpler kind of man might be able to use.

[32] as in Acts 26.23, R.V. margin.   [34] *Contra Celsum*, III, 24.
[33] *Dialogue with Trypho*, 85.   [35] VIII, 36.

E

For it is mostly people quite untrained who do this work.[36]

It may seem out of place to include, at some length, this material about exorcism, when this chapter is concerned with early missionary preaching. But all that was done in driving out demons seems to have been so essentially a proclaiming of the Gospel, that it is not to be thought of as mere accompaniment to, but itself a part of the preaching. Evidently it was a most popular part. Origen in that last quotation went out of his way to emphasize that it was done by 'the simpler kind of men', 'mostly people quite untrained'. There are signs that Origen is not most at home with this kind of thing. When he talks about the continued work of Christ, he himself most often chooses to speak of moral reformation. It is Celsus who has brought up the casting out of demons, and Origen is ill at ease. It is understandable. If one's days are spent in a theological college, it may not be easy suddenly to find it necessary to defend against a non-Christian's objections the chorus which the hot-gospeller is using to try to draw his crowd. That of which the scholarly Celsus complains may well remind us of the hot-gospeller:

We see also those who in the market-places make most disreputable displays and draw a crowd. They would not presume to approach a gathering of knowledgeable people nor among such make a display of their stuff. But whenever they see youngsters, and a mob of domestics, and a throng of witless folk, there they push themselves in and show off.[37]

What are the 'disreputable displays'? It seems they frequently form part of the Christian propaganda. With a crowd in the market-place before them, they do not only preach. They provide the 'word' with 'signs that follow'. They attack polytheism as the worship of demons; declare

their own Faith; boldly claim what it can do; and challenge
the crowd to give them a chance to prove it. Often the
chance is at hand. The consequent excitement of the crowd
the cultivated Celsus has seen, and it revolts him. Here is
a sample of preaching belonging to about Celsus' time, such
as he may have heard:

> Words so far. Now for a test case. Let someone be
> brought here before your judgment-seats, who is clearly
> demon-possessed. Bidden to speak by any Christian you
> like, this spirit, so surely as he pretends to deity else-
> where, will truly own himself a demon. . . . Mock as
> you will our Christ and His 'fables'—His resurrection,
> His ascension, His coming again to judge the world.
> Mock as you will—but get the demons to mock with you!
> Get them to deny that Christ will judge every soul of man
> from the world's beginning in a resurrection body! . . .
> Get them to deny that . . . they are bound for that same
> judgment day with all their worshippers and works!
> Why, all the authority and power we have over them is
> from naming the name of Christ, and reminding them
> of what threatens them from God at the hands of Christ.
> So at our touch and insufflation . . . they come out of
> bodies as we command, unwilling and distressed, and
> shamed before your eyes. . . . These testimonies of your
> gods have been a wonted means of making Christians,
> since by full belief in these, we believe in Christ as Lord.[38]

That is Tertullian of Carthage (c. 197). He is far from
being one 'of the simpler kind' and 'quite untrained'.
Compared with Origen, however, he is more at home with
the excitable, emotional, and extreme, and less concerned
in his teaching to make religion 'reasonable'. Two generations later we find Cyprian, Bishop of Carthage, declaring
that he preaches in the market-place in the very same way.

[38] Tertullian, *Apology*, 23. Notice that the creed as used here includes
'He shall come to judge the quick and the dead', or some words like
those.

He is greatly daring, for the final half-century of struggle between the Church and the pagan Empire is just beginning. To read his description, is almost to hear him preaching:

> I am a Christian. No need to wring the confession by torture. I avow it. Your gods? I do destroy them—not in remote and secret places—openly, publicly, in the very market-place where your magistrates and governors can hear. . . . By declaring myself a Christian in a crowded place, with the people standing around, I am confounding both you and your gods by a straightforward and public announcement.
>
> Why give your attention to the weakness of [a Christian's] body? Assail the vigour of his soul! Break his strength of mind! Destroy his faith! By discussion subdue him, subdue by reasoning—if you can! Or if your gods have anything of divinity and power, let them arise for their own vengeance! . . . Oh, would you but hear and see them when charged by us, cut with spiritual scourges, cast out from possessed bodies by torture of our words. As they feel the lashings and floggings they howl and groan at the voice of man and the power of God, and they confess that Judgment is to come. Come and see that what we say is true. And since yourselves say that such are the gods you worship, believe what they say! . . . You will see that we are besought by those whom you beseech, we are feared by those whom you fear, whom you adore. You will see that under our hand they stand bound, and tremble as captives, whom you admire and venerate as lords.[39]

We noticed that Origen seemed to be ill-at-ease about some of it; we confessed that most of us nowadays are uncomfortable about such phenomena. Here is a case of acute discomfort. A former student of mine, now a missionary in China, wrote to me in these terms:

[39] Cyprian *To Demetrianus*, 13, 15.

Cases of mental derangement, as you know, are frequent, and often the minister is sent for. My Chinese colleague goes with confidence. The sufferer in such a case himself believes his fits of madness to be possession by an evil spirit. The Chinese minister believes the same. He follows the apostolic pattern and in the name of Jesus bids the devil be gone—with some remarkable results. I feel outside all this. Both mental illness and mental health I think of in entirely other terms, and I feel no use to anybody. What am I to do?

Here is another case, not ending with a question, but with some measure of an answer. I give it in all essentials as it came to me from an Indian missionary who wrote a few days after the events described:

—— is a small town, with a mayor who is a leading member of the Congress Party, and extremely anti-British. The Mayor's daughter goes to the local government school, where the headmistress happens to be a Christian. The girl was taken ill; they had to tie her down in bed; she used to cry out that evil spirits were in her chest and throat and would not let her swallow. Everyone agreed that she was devil-possessed. This went on for ten days, and they could find nobody to help her. The family was called together. They performed the last rites according to the Sikh religion. The girl was about to die. Then someone said, 'We might let her teacher know.' So they sent to the Christian headmistress. This Indian lady had never been a very active Christian, never sought a chance to witness for Christ. Here she was, asked to visit this household and the mad girl. 'I was afraid of the evil spirits,' she said afterwards. 'I dared not go alone. Yet whom could I take with me? There seemed to be nobody, so I just prayed, and took the Bible.'

Notice, in this modern case, how a woman who knows nothing of the Early Church, spontaneously, almost inevitably, is brought to do the same things. In this record, the Bible, as that which contains true religion mightier than the false, is used exactly as we have seen those articles of the creed used in the early centuries. The account continues:

She stood beside the girl's bed, and prayed and prayed. She gripped the Bible hard as something which stood for a power greater than the evil spirits. Thinking like this she put the Bible down by the girl's pillow, and prayed again. What is this? A heathen charm round the girl's neck. That looks all wrong, she thought, with the Bible there. She took off the charm and burned it—a risky thing to do with the girl so close to death. . . . Within the hour the girl had quietened; for the first time she was able to take a little food. Then, still holding the Bible to her breast, she dropped to sleep and slept all night.

Next morning they sent word, ' She's worse '. ' What have you been doing to her? ' said the headmistress. ' Nothing,' they said. ' Well hardly anything. We just put another charm round her neck.' ' Take it off,' she ordered. They did, and the girl recovered. So it went on. To protect her against evil, the headmistress moved her to the school—and some non-Christian girls, and staff, thereupon moved out, for fear of evil spirits. Always with the Bible somewhere near, always surrounded by Christian prayer, the girl was soon completely recovered.

Now the results: It is the talk of the town. The headmistress cannot go out without people pointing to her. And everybody is asking, ' What is in that Book? ' Throughout the school, teachers and children are saying, ' Can we read it? ' The mayor himself has bought a copy, and another for his wife. The greatest change is in the headmistress. Instead of being only a nominal Christian, she has become an awe-inspired, faithful, praying woman. God chose one of the most significant families in the town—from a local point of view, the mayor's; from a national point of view, a leader of the Congress Party's; from a religious point of view, a family furthest removed from Christian influences. God performed this miracle through one of His weakest instruments. Surely there is a purpose.

If the above provided some measure of an answer to our difficulties, perhaps one further quotation may complete it. When European missionaries went back from internment camp to churches in China which for years had been left to Chinese leadership, they found some practices established which they themselves might never have set going, but with which they hesitated to try to interfere. Here is one such case, a case which it is good to remember in days when the Church in China must again stand alone. It is a church in a country town, with what it calls a ministry of healing:

> They admit that medicine is the healing gift of God. But there is no doctor in this town. What as Christians they have begun to do is this. After every Sunday morning service, they hold intercessions for church members who are sick. Sometimes non-Christians ask for their prayers. They go to their houses very willingly on two conditions: (1) that it is understood that they make no guarantee of a cure; (2) that the patient must try to believe in the power of God. They tell those who recover not to thank the people who prayed but to give glory to God. Quite a number seem to have become good Christians through the church's prayers for their sickness like this. One notable instance is Mr. Ko who was suffering from a mental complaint. The prayer and help of the church made a change in him which was a cure. For the last six years he has been a keen Christian. Frankly, I cannot see anything unsound in such theology.

Unsound theology? Surely not! This Younger Church is repeating the experience of the Early Church, and is true to the tradition both of apostolic and post-apostolic preaching.

III

PREACHING CHRIST

THE 'THREE STEPS' which we saw enumerated by
Lactantius (c. 320), and quite similarly by Origen (c. 250),
were, (1) negatively, the rejection of idols; (2) positively,
acceptance of the one true God; (3) learning of Jesus Christ.[1]
The first two steps are sufficiently illustrated by what we
have already considered of the attack upon polytheism, along
with that demonstration concerning gods false and true, so
frequently to be seen in exorcism. Both these sections of
our study we approached with misgivings: Was so ruthless
an attack the best approach to the heathen? Was the driving
out of devils 'sound theology'? The misgivings, as we
proceeded, may to some extent have been answered. Now
we come to 'Learning of Jesus Christ'. Perhaps we give a
sigh of relief, for we anticipate no misgivings here. But—
we had better not be too sure about that.

First let us notice, this third step is by no means fully
represented in every Apology, for the simple reason that in
some cases all time and energy are taken up making sure
of steps one and two. We shall first look at the preaching
of Christ by use of the scriptures. We shall include the
Jewish scriptures—ancient, established, authoritative. The
Christian preacher thinks of them, above all, as leading on

[1] See p. 54 above.

72

to Christ. And we shall go on to those more recent writings, among which the most important are the Four Gospels, the ' Memoirs of the Apostles ', Justin calls them. In church, as in the Jewish synagogue, sermons were essentially based upon scripture. This from Justin's *First Apology*[2] is one of the earliest descriptions:

> On the day called Sunday, there is a meeting for ' all in one place ', according to the city or the countryside where one lives. . . .

The phrase ' all in one place ' is the same as in Acts 2.1, and may be a conscious recollection of the beginning of the Church's progress, the Day of Pentecost.

> . . . The Memoirs of the Apostles or the Writings of the Prophets are read as long as there is time, and when the reader has ceased, the president in an address gives a reminder and a challenge to imitation of these good things.

We are here concerned with preaching to the heathen rather than with preaching in church. In such preaching what use, if any, was made of the scriptures?

We have to remember that books were few, and—almost as important and more easily overlooked—that rolls were more frequent than codices, and far harder to handle than mere turning of pages if you needed a casual reference. The Greek Old Testament was widely, though often vaguely known among educated Gentiles, but how often would there be a copy at hand to be perused? The writings which we call the New Testament were yet in process of coming together into the Canon. Would one be able to find in the town a set of all the twenty-seven? When all this is considered, it may well seem amazing that there is no single Apology we know, which does not refer to the scriptures,

[2] *I Apology*, 67; see also *Trypho*, 103, 106.

and either call men to search the scriptures for themselves,
or preach Christianity to men from scriptural texts. One
Apology seemed likely to prove an exception, the *Octavius*
of Minucius Felix. This Apology is limited to what we
have called the first two steps. For this reason the end of
the argument finds the heathen Caecilius just arrived at
monotheism, but not yet at a fully Christian position. The
two Christian friends who have won him over have not as
yet even mentioned Jesus Christ by name, still less made
any reference to the Gospels. Surely the usual argument
from prophecy, calling in the authority of the Jewish scriptures, would be lacking here. But no, here comes one paragraph which not only refers to the Old Testament, but seems
to require some knowledge of New Testament fulfilment
(in the rejection of the Messiah). Octavius is maintaining
that the destruction of Jerusalem in A.D. 70 does not mean
that the God of Israel is powerless before Rome.

> Read over carefully their scriptures—or Josephus if you
> prefer him—and you will know they deserved it. It had
> all been foretold if they continued in their obstinacy. You
> will then understand that they forsook before they were
> forsaken.[3]

The argument from prophecy is all but universally used by
the Apologists. Justin, for example, finds in the Old Testament the complete forecast of our Lord's birth, life, passion
and triumph. Isaiah 7.14 is the Annunciation:

> Behold a virgin shall conceive and bring forth a son,
> and shall say for his name 'God with us'.[4]

He accepts the Greek word for 'virgin' and seems quite
unconscious of the fact that the Hebrew original reads

---

[3] 33.

[4] *I Apology*, 33. This and all the following passages Justin uses both
in *I Apology* and in the *Trypho*. Trypho, of course, has difficulties with
some. In the case of Isa. 7.14 he is not slow to tell the indignant
Justin that 'the Scripture has " young woman " not " virgin " '.

' young woman '. Micah 5.2 ' But thou Bethlehem . . .'
foretells the birth. Justin, though he is a Gentile, was himself born at Neapolis, now Nablus, the ancient Shechem;
so he comments, ' Now there is a village in the land of the
Jews, 35 stadia from Jerusalem, where Jesus was born '.
Elsewhere he adds, ' a cave near the village '. Very likely,
for he was no more distant in either space or time, he knew
the actual spot as well as I know the birthplace of David
Livingstone.

Isa. 9.6 rejoices at His advent:

> For unto us a child is born, and unto us a young man is
> given, and the government is upon His shoulders.

' Which,' Justin adds, ' gives us a clue to the power of the
cross.'[5] He promises to enlighten us further about this in
a moment. When we get to it you may judge if it is
enlightenment. We shall not be surprised that Isa. 35.6
points Justin, as it does ourselves, to our Lord's mighty
acts. But failing to verify his references, Justin's memory
betrays him into a mixture of Isaiah with what can only be
recollection of Luke 7.22:

> At His coming the lame shall leap as an hart, and the
> tongue of the stammerer shall be clear speaking: the
> blind shall see, and the lepers shall be cleansed; and
> the dead shall rise, and walk about.[6]

Gen. 49.11, strange-worded prophecy of Judah's peace and
plenty, is for Justin clear indication of our Lord's triumphal
entry into Jerusalem, and the shedding of His cleansing
blood:

> Binding his foal unto the vine, and washing his robe in
> the blood of the grapes.

He seems fond of this, since twice in the *First Apology* and
twice again in the *Trypho* he brings it in.[7] The same

[5] 35.   [6] 48.   [7] 32, 54; *Trypho*, 52-54 (and 120).

repetition applies to the next two quotations. Isa. 65.2 he regards as 'The Spirit of prophecy speaking in the person of Christ'. That is why this passage says, 'I have spread out my hands to a disobedient and gainsaying people', meaning Christ's arms outstretched on the cross.[8] And so with Ps. 22 about the mocking, casting of lots for His vesture, piercing of His hands and His feet.[9] Ps. 3.5 means His death and resurrection:

> I laid me down and slept, and rose again, because the Lord sustained me.[10]

And here comes that to which Justin was referring concerning 'the power of the cross'. He quotes the triumphant Ps. 96, up to verse 10, 'The Lord reigneth'. Then he continues the sentence with what can only be an early Christian gloss, one never of wide acceptance, 'The Lord hath reigned *from the tree*'. In the *Trypho* (73) he lashes the Jews with indignant words, for cutting this out of their scriptures, saying to have done so is worse than the golden calf, sacrificing their children or slaying the prophets.[11] Oh if only he had been initiated into textual criticism! Did we promise ourselves that in this section we should find no cause for misgivings?

This may seem to be an extraordinary way to use the scriptures in preaching to the heathen. Proof-texts from scriptures which the heathen little knows, and which, to the knowing, could not have proved at all! There is much that must make us feel uncomfortable. Which of us has not felt discomfort sometimes on hearing preachers announce

[8] 38, 49; *Trypho*, 97, 114.
[9] 35, 38; *Trypho*, 97, 104.
[10] 38.
[11] 41; *Trypho*, 73. This gloss is unknown in any surviving Greek version. Besides Justin it is quoted among Greek writers only in the *Epistle of Barnabas* 8, and is perhaps less directly referred to by Irenaeus, *Against Heresies*, V, 17. It is to be found in the Old Latin Version, *Psalterium Romanum*. From Tertullian (*To the Jews* 10, where, he, too, connects it with Isa. 9.6, 'the government shall be upon his shoulder') onwards, it is well used by Latin Fathers.

their texts, especially texts from the Old Testament? And then, often, the sermon has turned out to be much sounder than the verse of scripture on which it has been made to hang. With Justin, and preachers as early as he, there is this much to be said: They seek a scriptural basis for what they are saying, especially for what they are saying about Jesus Christ. That this is the criterion, we can soon see by the way Justin uses the Old Testament in his *First Apology*. He quotes 114 verses; 53 are from Isaiah and 41 from the Psalms. That accounts for 94 of the 114. There are 7 verses from Genesis; the rest are little more than isolated verses from another nine books. Why this selection? Isaiah[12] and the Psalter have always been the books which Christians have felt, and feel still, to be Messianic. The Old Testament is used almost exclusively as pointing to Him.

The claims to be made for the Lord Jesus Christ are so immense that they need, not just these new 'Memoirs of the Apostles', but the independent backing of ancient scriptures. This is how Justin puts it:

We will now produce the proof, not taking it on trust from those who say so, but being inevitably persuaded by those who prophesied before it came to pass, since we see with our eyes things happened, and happening, just as they were foretold. This, we think, will seem to you also the best and truest evidence. . . . In these Books of the Prophets we find announced as coming, one born of a Virgin; and growing to manhood; and healing every disease and sickness and raising the dead; and being hated, disowned, and crucified—Jesus our Christ; and dying and rising again, and ascending into heaven, both being, and being called, Son of God; and certain sent by Him to every race of men to preach these things, and its being the men from the Gentiles rather, who believe in Him.[13]

[12] 34 out of the 53 are from Deutero-Isaiah, and 14 from Chapter 1.
[13] 30, 31. See also 53.

Not all that Justin has on this list did we include in the passages chosen to illustrate his use of the Old Testament.

There is one, however, which ought not to be omitted by any of us who believes, with Justin, that the Universal Church *is* the fulfilment of that destiny which the old Israel refused:

> When as prophesying those things which are to happen, the prophetic Spirit says this, ' Out of Zion shall go forth a law, and a word of the Lord from Jerusalem and he judges in the midst of the nations, and shall rebuke much people. And they shall beat their swords into plough-shares and their spears into pruning hooks. Nation shall not lift up sword against nation, neither shall they learn war any more '—even so it has come to pass, as you can be persuaded. For from Jerusalem there did go out men, twelve in number, into the world, and these unlearned, and with no ability in speech. And in the power of God they proclaimed to every race of men that they were sent by the Christ to teach to all the word of God. And we who formerly used to kill one another, not only do not make war on our enemies, but, rather than lie and deceive our inquisitors, willingly die confessing the Christ.[14]

Something has happened, so big that it must have the biggest backing. In seeking scriptural authority, Christianity, the child of Judaism, is again showing itself true to type. The Christian preacher does right to seek a scriptural authority, though sometimes he may do wrong to history, to his texts, to reason itself, in his search. The trouble is that the New Testament writings are not yet venerable, accepted, known—not yet scripture. Second-century preachers therefore seek their scriptural authority too much in the Prophets and the Psalter, basing some things where you and I can no longer think of their being able to stand. As we read these Old Testament passages, some of them forced into strange new duties—the Virgin who conceives,

[14] 39.

Bethlehem Ephrathah, 'binding his foal unto the vine',
'I spread out my hands to a disobedient people', 'the Lord
reigned from the tree'—we need to remember that what
Justin cares about is the fact of the annunciation, and the
birth at Bethlehem; the fact of the ministry of mighty
works, and the triumphal entry on Palm Sunday; the fact
of the crucifixion, and the fact that it did not mean defeat
but that He comes to reign. These are the facts that he
reads back into the scriptures, but he holds them first as
facts. The New Testament documents will put these facts
into the scriptures, more effectively than Justin has been
able to do—by those documents becoming scriptures themselves. And then Christians will have that which Justin
rightly longed for, a Bible to preach from.

It seems as though, both in the second century and in
the twentieth, the way of the missionary with regard to
the Old Testament has been to swing to one extreme or the
other, either excessive use, or almost total neglect. There
are missionaries to-day who try to make the Old Testament
bear more than it is safe to base upon it. There are more
who, recognizing its complexity, and fearing that wayfar-
ing men might err therein, use the Old Testament not at
all in missionary preaching, sparingly in the training of
their converts, and still inadequately in the life of the young
Church.[15] If in the second century Justin represents excessive use, it is his contemporary, the writer to Diognetus,
who represents complete neglect. In passing we may recall
that this Diognetus is quite possibly the tutor to Marcus
Aurelius, addressed here as 'exceedingly anxious to understand the religion of the Christians'. The *Epistle to
Diognetus* couples Jewish 'sacrifices of blood and fat and
whole-burnt-offerings' with the superstitions of the heathen.
It says their observances with regard to clean and unclean
meats, Sabbath, circumcision, and the sacred seasons, mark
the 'vanity, error, excessive fussiness, and pretensions of

[15] See Godfrey Phillips *The Old Testament in the World Church*, Chaps.
2 and 3.

the Jews'. Not only does it leave out that almost universal argument from prophecy, but it refers to the Old Testament not at all. Notice, however, that in the second century such an attitude is the exception; it is on Justin's side that we find the rule. This is worthy of notice because, in taking Christianity to a heathen land, a missionary might well feel that Jewish scriptures have, after all, a limited service to perform. The Old Testament has contributions to make which are not repeated in the New, to steps one and two, the rejection of idols, and acceptance of the one true God. When one proceeds to step three, teaching about Jesus Christ, are the heathen necessarily interested in our Lord as the fulfilment of Jewish expectations? What they want to know is rather how He answers their own needs. Besides the line of religious development represented by Judaism, the world into which these early missionaries went contained altars and temples, myths and oracles, aspirations of mystic and philosopher. Was there anything here which Christ came to fulfil? It was soon evident that a preacher to the heathen who would get his message home, must think not only of the scriptures which he might bring, but of a point of contact with all that his hearers brought. For a missionary of the second century, what could compare, as a point of contact, with the widespread philosophic conception of the *Logos* (Word)?

Perhaps I am in a better position than many to understand, for during my fifteen years in China I knew what it was to stand in a similar situation with regard to pre-Christian thought there. *Tao* is 'the Way'—the Way all things were made, Itself before all things; the Moral Order, the Way men should live, Itself the incomparable Good. And—surely at this point the New Testament translators were inspired—there in the Chinese of St. John's Gospel it stands:

In the beginning was the *Tao,* and the *Tao* was with *Shang-ti,* and the *Tao* was *Shang-ti*. All things were made by Him. . . . And the *Tao* became flesh and dwelt among us.

What a point of contact! It has its dangers, of course. The greatest danger to missionary preaching is that the missionary should be so intent on a point of contact on the heathen side, that he may lose sight of that which is transcendent on the side of the religion which he brings. This is the strength of the preaching represented by the *Epistle to Diognetus.* This missionary may unduly neglect Christ's fore-runners; he is at least satisfyingly sure of Christ's uniqueness:

> For this is no discovery on earth which has been handed on to the Christians, nor an invention of mortals which they thus think it right carefully to observe, nor a dispensation of human mysteries with which they have been entrusted. Truly God Himself, almighty, all-creating, and invisible, Himself from heaven has sent the Truth and the *Logos,* holy and incomprehensible, and set Him firm in their hearts. He did not, as man might have guessed, send some attendant or angel or ruler, or one of those who manage earth's affairs, or of those entrusted with the administration of heaven, but the Artificer Himself, the Creator of all things, by Whom He made the heavens, by Whom He enclosed the sea in its proper bounds, Whose mysteries all the elements faithfully observe, through Whom the sun received the measure of the daily course he keeps, Whose call to shine at night the moon obeys. . . . Him sent He to them. Was it then, as human reckoning might have it, in despotism, and fear and terror? No indeed, but in gentleness and meekness, as a King He sent His kingly Son. He sent Him as God sent Him as Man to men. As saving He sent, as persuading and not to force. For force does not belong to God. As calling He sent, not pursuing. As loving He sent, not judging. For He shall send Him judging, and who shall stand His coming?[16]

[16] 7.

Translating those words, it seemed that, here was a man
who had begun, as it were, to preach on the Prologue to
St. John's Gospel, choosing his text because the heathen (the
tutor of Marcus Aurelius?) would be at home with the idea
of *Logos,* and through *Logos* might come to 'only-begotten
Son'. And then as the preacher gets to 'only-begotten Son'
(it is there in the last verse, 18, of the Prologue), he finds
himself preaching on John 3.16, not because of what the
heathen will be at home with, but because the Gospel is
just that.

Looking again, is it too much to bring in John 3.16? Is
there enough about atonement here? Yet this preacher
does go on in the next stage of his discourse to expound the
atonement, in language which if not Johannine, is
definitely scriptural. Pauline, we might say, for he is clearly
paraphrasing what St. Paul writes about 'all having sinned
and fallen short of the glory of God',[17] and what God did
for sinners 'when the fulness of the time came'.[18] And
Petrine next, for he goes on to use the word of Mark 10.45
—and Mark means Peter—that Christ was given 'a ran-
som'; and to quote the great phrase of I Peter 3.18 'the
Righteous for the unrighteous.'

Pauline—Petrine—Johannine: Thinking like this I read
on:

For God loved men, for whom He made the world, . . .
      to whom He gave reason (*logos*) . . .
      to whom He sent His only begotten
      Son,
      to whom He promised the kingdom
      which is in heaven.

And then suddenly I saw it, and realized that that first
impression, that from the Prologue the preacher had moved
on to John 3.16, was not wrong. For here in the last stage
of his discourse, the actual words of John 3.16 will no longer

[17] Rom. 3.23, etc.   [18] Gal. 4.4.

be kept back. Word for word the same in the Greek, and occurring in the same order, can there be any doubt that this passage was here uppermost in his mind? I print the relevant words in capitals:

> FOR GOD LOVED men for whom He made THE WORLD . . .
> to whom HE GAVE reason (*logos*) . . . to whom He sent
> HIS ONLY BEGOTTEN SON, to whom He promised the king-
> dom which is in heaven (=eternal life).[19]

If he began by preaching to the philosopher, he ends by just preaching the Gospel.

We cannot spend long listening to Justin as a New Testament preacher, yet we must not entirely neglect him as such, since his writings form a landmark in the development of the New Testament Canon. No one can read his *First Apology* without being struck by the frequent and spontaneous recital, to be paralleled in so many of the early Apologies, of the main facts of the life of our Lord, just as they are to become embodied in the later Creed. After dwelling on other doctrine, he suddenly breaks out:

> Our Teacher of these things is Jesus Christ,
> who was born for this purpose,
> and was crucified under Pontius Pilate.[20]

And again:

> Jesus Christ our Teacher
> was crucified
> and died
> and rose again
> and ascended into heaven.[21]

---

[19] The words 'sent the Son' occur in John 3.17 and 'sent His only begotten Son' in I John 4.9, so this phrase would easily come to mind as, subconsciously, he avoids the repetition of 'gave', just used. 'Kingdom of heaven' is in the Synoptic Gospels the equivalent of 'eternal life' in the Fourth Gospel and is so used here. Lightfoot's text marks 'For God loved' as John 3.16, and 'He sent His only-begotten Son' as I John 4.9. He does not mark 'He gave', nor remark about this synonym of 'eternal life'.

[20] *I Apology*, 13.   [21] 21; see also 42, 46.

The longest list of all has already been quoted. It departs from the usual credal pattern and is much more Justin's own summary:

> Born of a Virgin,
> growing to manhood,
> healing every disease and sickness and raising the dead,
> being hated, disowned, and crucified,
>   Jesus our Christ;
> dying,
> and rising again,
> and ascending into heaven
> being, and being called, the Son of God,
> the Apostles going to every race,
> believers being the Gentiles rather.[22]

Not only does this missionary often recite these basic New Testament facts. In this Apology he quotes from the New Testament something like 46 verses.[23] They are *all* from the Gospels, and they are from all four. Matthew predominates with 41 verses; Mark has one, Luke three, and John one. His preference for Matthew is because Matthew, like Justin himself, makes frequent use of the *Testimonies*, Christian collections of Old Testament texts. Of the 41 verses from Matthew, 28 (nearly 70 per cent) come from the Sermon on the Mount.

I have had occasion to spend much time, not only (as now) studying the early missionary preaching in the Roman Empire, but the earliest in the Chinese Empire. The date when that began was 635, the same year in which St. Aidan journeyed from Iona to Lindisfarne. These much more travel-stained monks from Persia, arriving in China's capital in 635, were set (the Chinese inscription tells us) to translate their scriptures in the Imperial Library, so that the Emperor might decide whether or no to issue a toleration

[22] 31.
[23] It is sometimes difficult to know where to draw the line between a reference and a quotation.

edict—which, as a matter of fact, they did so earn in 638.
Contrast that with the furtive work of Justin and the rest
—writing to their Emperor, it is true, but more likely to
ornament his amphitheatre than his library.

We need not envy them the library overmuch. Its
200,000 volumes were in the Chinese language which they
could not yet read. What was worse, they had only three
years to learn enough Chinese to translate something of
their scriptures, and that when no one before them had
faced the question of Christian terminology in Chinese, not
even the Chinese name for the Christian's God. Theirs
was of course an impossible task. The Chinese they wrote,
strangely surviving sealed up in a cave in north-west China
all these long centuries, is barbarous and all but unintelli-
gible. The chief value it has is to show what men, taking
the Gospel for the first time to one quarter of the human
race, themselves so wretchedly equipped for the task, felt
they must struggle to get into Chinese. The chief item is
a Life of Christ:

The Virgin birth,
the visit to the Temple at the age of twelve,
the Baptism and descent of the Spirit,
the ministry of healing and teaching,
the plotting of His enemies,
the betrayal, charge, arrest, trial before Pilate,
death ' on the tree ',
Resurrection and Ascension,
Pentecost,
retribution to Judas and the Jews,
the spread of Christianity through the Roman Empire
    and to Persia.[24]

Most of this story is in outline. Twice however, in spite of
language difficulty, they come to verse-for-verse translation.
The two passages are, Mat. 6.1 to 7.20; and Mat. 27.57 to
28.20. Again it is Matthew's Gospel; and this time 60 per

[24] See John Foster, *The Church of the T'ang Dynasty*, 48f.

cent is from the Sermon on the Mount. The rest is an even nobler choice, the Resurrection appearances.

At both ends of the world the early missionary preaching was as similar as that. Irenaeus, Bishop of Lyons, belonged to Asia Minor before he came to Gaul, so he had personal knowledge of a wide stretch of the second-century Church. We can read his words with thoughts that go wider still, thinking not only, as he would, of Greek and Latin, but of Syriac and Chinese too:

> This preaching, as cited, and this Faith, as forementioned, the Church although scattered in the whole world, diligently guards as if it lived in one house, and believes, like the above, as if it had but one mind and the same heart, and preaches and teaches and hands on these things harmoniously, as if it had got one mouth. And although there are different languages in the world, the force of the tradition is one and the same.[25]

Teaching about Jesus Christ—for we are still occupied with that third of the 'three steps'—to those outside the company of believers can never depend on documents alone. It needs the support of evidence from life. From the time of the Apostles onward, preaching to the heathen has included, (1) witness to one's own conversion; (2) demonstration of the Christian life; (3) the attraction of the Christian community; (4) the testimony of success. These are all aspects of the life of the Church.

1. *Witness to one's own conversion:* It is no accident that in the Acts there is one story which is told three times over, the conversion of Saul of Tarsus.[26] How often on their missionary journeys St. Luke must have heard him tell it. How often, as we read the Epistles, we hear him tell parts of it again: 'But when it was the good pleasure of God to reveal His Son in me.' . . .[27] 'I knew a man in Christ.' . . .[28] 'O wretched man that I am, who shall

[25] Irenaeus, *Against Heresies,* I, 10.　　[27] Gal. 1.15f.
[26] Acts 9, 22, 26.　　[28] II Cor. 12.2.

deliver me? I thank God, through Jesus Christ our Lord.'[29]
Some reference peeps out of almost every epistle. He must
have been always referring to it. This is true of other
missionaries, true in the second century and the third.
Justin, Tatian, Theophilus, Gregory Thaumatourgos, and
Cyprian have left us in some detail accounts of their conversion. Irenaeus, Tertullian and Clement of Alexandria
give us a picture, if not much detail. And all do it in such
a way that, even if in its present context it is not preaching
to the heathen (in many cases it *is*), one can well imagine
its being so used.

With Justin, Tatian, and Theophilus, conversion follows
a philosopher's search for truth, which ends when truth
is approached through the Old Testament prophets, at once
more venerable and more satisfying than the teachers of
Greek wisdom; and they lead on to Christ. Let Tatian
represent these: He tells that he had examined Greek
thought, even been initiated into a Mystery Cult, and wit-
nessed the debased religion of the temples at Rome. It
was then that Justin converted him:

> With my thoughts bent upon these weighty themes, I
> chanced to come across certain barbarian scriptures, too
> old to compare with the teaching of Greeks, too divine to
> compare with their error. I came to put my trust in these,
> because there was no conceit about their style, nor any-
> thing artificial about the speakers, the composition of it
> all was easy to understand, things to come were fore-
> known, the messages given beyond expectation, and all
> things had one guiding principle. And, my soul taught
> of God, I understood that there are some things which
> tend towards condemnation, but others which set free
> from the bondage that is in the world, and snatch us from
> rulers many, aye from ten thousand tyrants.[30]

No one who has known life in a land where ten thousand
devils rule will question the reality of this experience of

[29] Rom. 7.24f.   [30] *Address to the Greeks*, 29.

release. If you call it 'intellectual conversion' do not therefore think lightly of it, nor forget that in these men moral
regeneration is never overlooked, and none of these accounts
lacks emotion. Gregory Thaumatourgos is similar, though
when converted he is not a full-blown philosopher but a
freshman just come up for study in Caesarea. Chance
brings him to sit at the feet of Origen:

> Like some spark it came dropping into my inmost soul,
> and there, being kindled and catching fire, was love:
> Love towards the Word (*Logos*) Himself . . . the most
> lovely, and towards this man, His friend and repre-
> sentative.[31]

Cyprian's concern was not the quest for truth, but the sense
of sin, and doubting the possibility of starting anew; of
this he told, to try to convert Donatus in like manner:

> While I was still lying in darkness and gloomy night,
> tossing in the sea of this world, floundering this way and
> that, and wavering on a blundering course, knowing
> nothing of my own life, a stranger to truth and light, I
> used to think it difficult—as my manner of life then was,
> utterly distasteful, [to believe], what the tenderness of
> God was offering me for my salvation, that it should be
> possible for anyone to be born anew, and in the washing
> of water be quickened to new life. 'How,' I would con-
> tend, 'is such a conversion possible? . . . It is inevit-
> able . . . as it always has been, that a drunken thirst
> should invite, that pride should puff me up, bad temper
> inflame me, greed disturb, cruelty thrill, ambition delight,
> and lust hurry me towards ruin, with allurements that
> will not let go.'
>   Thus often, to myself. For I was involved in such a
> mass of errors from my earlier life, and they were holding
> me. I did not even myself believe that I could win free.
> So I got into the way of showing compliance to my cling-
> ing vices, and, in despair of better things, I would

[31] *Address to Origen.*

applaud my badness as, after all, my own, belonging to me.

Then came the water of regeneration, and the stain of my past life was wiped away. A light from above, both bright and clear, shed itself upon my heart, now reconciled. Then, by the Spirit breathed from heaven, a second birth made me anew, a different man, and in a wonderful way: What in me had wavered, now stood firm; what had been shut tight, now opened; dark places shone; ease was given to what before seemed difficult; what I had deemed impossible, I could do.'[32]

Clement of Alexandria's conversion is usually thought of as that of a philosopher finding truth at last. He describes this experience, telling of the privilege he had of contact with outstanding men who 'preserved the tradition straight from Peter and James, John and Paul', influences from many quarters, including Tatian the Assyrian. One he puts above all, and probably he means Pantaenus:

When I chanced upon the last (but he was first in power), hunting him down hidden away in Egypt, then I came to rest.[33]

There are however other passages, containing less of philosophic quest, and more of the experience of re-birth:

Those who are still unbelievers are named (in Eph 2.3) children of wrath, brought up in wrath. But we are no more nurslings of wrath, who have been snatched from wandering, and are hastening to the truth. In this way then we who were once sons of lawlessness, through the kindness[34] of the Word (*Logos*) have now become sons of God. . . .[35]

[32] *To Donatus*, 3, 4.   [33] *Miscellanies*, I,1.

[34] As in Tit. 3.4, where it happens that there immediately follows the passage about 'washing of regeneration', to which Cyprian, in the preceding quotation, has referred.

[35] *Exhortation to the Heathen*, 2. It may be, of course, that the preacher is identifying himself with fellow-believers, without necessarily describing his own personal experience. But there is an element in it that he shares.

Rejoicing greatly and renouncing our old sentiments, we become young again for salvation, singing together in that psalmed prophecy:

> How good is God to Israel,
> To such as are upright in heart. . . .

The Word rescues man from the manner of life which is worldly, of common upbringing, and trains him for the salvation which is of faith towards God, a special upbringing.[36]

Irenaeus we may class, in the matter of conversion, along with Gregory Thaumatourgos. He speaks as though he were brought to a decision while a boy through contact with a man of apostolic stature. As he tells it he recaptures his hero-worship, much as the still youthful Gregory pours out his enthusiasm for his teacher Origen. This, Irenaeus himself explains, with the penetrating remark that the experiences of boyhood are recalled more easily than those of yesterday because they have entered into the soul, grown with it, and become a part of it. That is why he can now describe the place and all about it, see again the blessed Polycarp sitting there discoursing (a preacher would sit— it was the early custom), remember his way of life, his looks, the sermons he preached to the people:

> And he used to talk away of his intercourse with John, and with the rest of those who had seen the Lord. He would recall their sayings and this and that which he had heard from them about the Lord, about His mighty works, and His teaching. . . . These things even then, since the mercy of God was upon me, I used to listen to eagerly, noting them for remembrance not on paper but in my very heart. And ever since, by God's grace, I literally go ruminating upon them.[37]

[36] *Paidagogos*, opening paragraph.
[37] The verb is 'chew the cud'; he means 'go over them again and again'. Quoted by Eusebius, *Ecclesiastical History*, V, 20.

The way of Tertullian is to be, not always brief, but always
to the point. With regard to his conversion he is both:

> The kind of men which we also ourselves were in the past,
> blind, without the light of the Lord. . . . Sinner though
> I be of every kind, I was born for nothing save repent-
> ance.[38]

That is how he preached about repentance. Is there any
better way to preach?

2. *Demonstration of the Christian life:* For this type of
preaching the Apologists provide us with an embarrassment
of riches: they team with claims to a new standard of
morality achieved. Their confidence in appealing to what
the heathen know for themselves about the Christian life
is something to put over against the charges that Christians
ate babies and had nocturnal feasts marked by sexual
promiscuity. These caricatures of the Eucharist and Agape
can seldom have been taken seriously unless by the lowest
dregs of the mob.

In cruel times, the voice of the Christian preacher is
sometimes itself strident. This is the challenging way in
which Tertullian preached about Christian living:

> We are arraigned under still another allegation, said to
> be a dead loss (*infructuosi*) to business. How can that be
> of men living alongside you, with the same food, clothing,
> equipment, and the same needs in order to live? For we
> are neither Brahmins nor Fakirs of the Indians, forest-
> dwellers, banished from life. We remember that we owe
> thanks to God the Lord of creation, and no fruit of works
> of His do we refuse—watching, of course, against mis-
> use and excess. And so we share daily life, in the square,
> among the stalls, at the baths, the shops, the factories, at
> inns, on your market-days, and in all the rest of com-
> merce. We sail and fight and farm and trade, we and
> you together. Similarly we join in works of skill, our

[38] *On Repentance*, 1, 12. But see also *To Scapula*, 1, 5, and *Apology*,
50, where he speaks of the converting power of the martyrs.

contribution at your service. How we can seem a dead
loss to your business, in which and for which we spend
our lives, I fail to realize.

If I do not attend your worship, I am none the less a
fellow-man. I do not, at the Saturnalia, take a nightly
bath (for fear of spoiling both night and day!); but I do
wash at the proper healthy time, as suits my warmth and
health. Enough to be stiff and cold after lustrations,
when I'm a corpse! I do not publicly take my place at
table at the Spring Festival, as the custom is with gladia-
tors at their final feast; but I do dine, wherever I am,
from your plenty. I buy no garland for my head. Does
it matter to you what I do with the flowers, so long as
they are sold out? For my part I prefer them not tied
up, but loose and waving everywhere, but if made into
a wreath, that *we* appreciate with noses—there may be
those who smell through their hair! No, we do not go
with you to the shows. However, things sold there to the
crowds, if I were to want them, I should buy more
cheaply in their proper places. Obviously we do not buy
incense. If parts of Arabia grumble, let the Sabaeans
know that their wares, of greater quantity and price, are
used up by Christians needing burial rather than gods
needing fumigations.

'At any rate,' you say, 'the temple revenues dwindle
every day—how many are there who still pay temple
dues?' Come, we are hardly up to bringing aid to beg-
gars, human and (those of yours) divine! Nor do we
consider giving alms except to those who ask. Let Jupiter
then hold out his hand and receive! Meanwhile our
charity spends more from street to street than does your
religion temple-going.

Taxes of another kind, however, may well express
obligation to the Christians. For the conscience that
keeps them from defrauding any other, makes them pay
what they owe. Go into it, how much is lost to the
Treasury by fraud and lying in your income tax returns.

It is a calculation easily to be made. And complaints on one side will be made up by compensations on the rest of the accounts.

I am open to confess that there are some, indeed in a position to complain, that they get small profit from the Christians. First pimps, procurers, those who haunt the baths. Next assassins, poisoners, magicians. Likewise fortune-tellers, diviners and astrologers. To be dead loss to these is surely living gain.[39]

The good life is a rebuke to evildoers, and sometimes it may be necessary to preach like that. But the good life is winsome too, and is it not better preaching to appeal? We noted before that Justin quotes large sections of the Sermon on the Mount. His introduction to this is as follows:

We who used formerly to find our pleasures in fornication, now kiss Chastity alone. We who used magical arts, have devoted ourselves to the good and unbegotten God. We who loved more than anything being men of means, now bring what we have to a common fund and communicate to the needy. We were haters and murderers of one another; and when it came to foreigners, with different social customs, we could not make a common home. But now since the revelation of Christ we share the same manner of life, we pray for our enemies, and seek to win over those who unjustly hate us. Lest you should think that we are just making a case, here are a few of Christ's teachings. And as mighty Kings[40] do you make enquiries whether we have been truly taught and truly teach.[41]

I recall hearing Azariah, Bishop of Dornakal, whose diocese grew in his twenty-five years as bishop to almost a quarter of a million outcaste Christians, tell how he used to teach

[39] *Apology*, 42, 43.
[40] Antoninus Pius, his son, and ' the senate and people of Rome ', are addressed in Justin's *First Apology*.
[41] *I Apology* 14.

recent converts to give their witness. 'I used to have them place their hands on their heads as if in the act of baptism, and repeat after me: I am a baptized Christian. Woe is me if I preach not the Gospel.' When one of us protested that these were illiterate outcastes—how could they preach?—'I will tell you,' said the Indian bishop. 'A caste villager asked one of our outcastes: "Have you seen God?" He answered, "Sir, you knew me two years ago. I was a drunkard. You know me now. I do not think I should have all this change if I had not seen Jesus Christ." Is there any better way,' concluded the bishop, 'of witnessing for God?' The answer in the early centuries and to-day is one.

3. *The attraction of the Christian Community:* These early writers seldom refer to 'a Christian'. It is impossible, e.g., for Justin, in the passage quoted above, to speak three sentences before he gets to the Christian community. Many previous quotations, therefore, touch upon this subject. One of the most attractive pictures of the Christian community is given in the *Epistle to Diognetus* 5 and 6, with its glorious paradoxes: Christians are here on earth but their citizenship is in heaven; they are put to death yet have the tokens of life; they are poor yet make many rich:

In a word, what soul is in body, this Christians are in the world. The soul is spread through all the parts of the body; so are Christians through all the cities of the world. The soul lives in the body, but is not of the body; so Christians live in the world, but are not of the world. . . . The soul is shut up in the body, but itself holds the body together; so too Christians are held down in the world as in a prison, yet it is they who hold the world together. . . . The soul when it is illtreated as to food and drink, does the better; so Christians when they are punished increase daily more and more. So great is the position to which God has appointed them, one which it is not lawful for them to refuse.

Aristides, with more practical detail, says the same thing. Christians have the commandments of Christ written in their hearts, and keep them:

> . . . looking forward to a resurrection of the dead and life of the world to come. . . . He who has, provides extra without reproach for him who has not. If they see a stranger, they bring him in to shelter, and rejoice over him as a very brother, for they call one another brethren. . . . And they are ready to lay down their lives for the sake of Christ.

He describes how, when one of them dies, they rejoice and give thanks to God, and:

> . . . escort his body, as one setting out on a journey. . . . Verily then this is the way of truth which leads its wayfarers to the everlasting kingdom. . . . Great and wondrous are the sayings *and deeds* of the Christians.[42]

One of the boldest words comes from Origen in answer to the heathen taunt that Palestine is a sordid corner for the one revelation of the Son of God. It is not, says Origen, one Man in one corner, but a movement which, beginning there, has extended to the world.

> If anyone desires to see many bodies filled with a divine spirit, ministering to the salvation of men everywhere, in a spirit like Christ's, let him take note of those who preach the Gospel of Jesus in all lands. . . . There are many Christs in the world. . . . Christ is the Head of the Church, so that Christ and the Church form one body. . . . From the Head to the very hem of the garment there is something of Christ.[43]

[42] *Apology of Aristides*, 15, 16. The passage about funerals is found in the Syriac only, 15.

[43] *Contra Celsum*, VI, 79 (abbreviated). A fanciful play upon the meaning of ' Christ ' (Anointed), causes him to see a type of Christ in the anointing of Aaron, and the reference in Psalm 133 to the oil running down his beard and even to the skirt of his garments. The fanciful exposition does not affect the truth of that to which Origen bears witness, as summarized in the last sentence of the quotation.

Origen does not idealize the Church. In another passage he refers to some bishops who 'lead indolent lives'. In still another he acknowledges that unhappy divisions do exist, a scandal to the heathen.[44] He knows ignorant Christians, nominal Christians, heretical Christians. That is why he talks about 'to the very hem of the garment'. The glory of the Church is the Headship of Christ, and its truest representatives those who stand nearest to the Head.

4. *The Testimony of Success:* All Christians have all the time agreed that God's purpose in creation shall not be finally defeated; and that His triumph shall be demonstrated here. Christians have often divided on the further question—How? Some are so placed that they can see God's triumph only in contrast to the present, a coming in the clouds of heaven, neither helped nor hindered by these happenings on earth. It is for us only to believe and suffer and wait. Some speak as though the New Testament were written wholly under such conditions. This is not so. St. Luke could plan his history to mark the stages of a progress, 'in Jerusalem, and in all Judaea and Samaria, and unto the uttermost part of the earth',[45] and see some sort of climax in St. Paul's arrival, even as a prisoner, at the world's capital. St. Paul himself in his imprisonment in Rome had a desire to depart and be with Christ—yet, 'I am in a strait betwixt the two'. He was a fighter, loved the ongoing cause, gloried in his outposts planted strategically to claim the future of the Mediterranean world. So it is later: In the worst times of persecution there are some able to look out as well as up; able too to tell the heathen what is happening and to happen, as Christ, through His servants, continues all that He began both to do and to teach. Such a faith in a present ongoing cause they claim itself to be a pointer to the End when the triumph will be complete:

Do you not see them, flung to the wild beasts to make

44 *Contra Celsum*, III, 10, 30.   45 Acts 1.8.

them deny their Lord, but unconquered? Do you not
see that the more there are who are punished, the more
the remainder increase? These things look not like the
achievements of men. They are the power of God. They
are the proofs of His coming.[46]

This, from the *Epistle to Diognetus,* must make us recall
that saying of Tertullian's which, usually *mis*quoted, has
become a proverb: 'The blood of Christians is seed.' He
is a grim figure of otherworldly mien. Concerning that
other world, he loves to preach hell-fire. So might you if
you had seen what he saw happen in North Africa. Yet it
is in his preaching that we hear the boldest claims for the
triumph of the cause in the second century:

We are of yesterday. Yet we have filled everything of
yours, cities, tenements, fortresses, towns, markets, the
very camps, divisions, companies, palace, senate, forum.
We have left you only the temples. We can estimate
your armies; in a single province they might be more.[47]
Despite inequality as to troops for what war should we
not be both capable and ready, we who so willingly face
slaughter, if it were not preferred, according to this
discipline of ours, to let us be slain rather than let us slay?
We could, both unarmed and without insurrection, join
battle with you by just going on strike,[48] by ill-will leading to a mere walk-out. For if we, so great a force of men,
were to break off from you for some shore at the world's
end, it would surely cover your empire with shame for
loss of so many citizens, of whatever kind, yes, and the

[46] *Epistle to Diognetus,* 7.
[47] Some translators seem to have forced the meaning that Christian
numbers in a single province would exceed the Roman legions. The natural
interpretation seems to be admission that pagans do outnumber Christians.
What is surprising is the claim which follows that there are by this time
many local majorities of Christians.
[48] *tantummodo discordes,* 'only (being) out of harmony'. I was
tempted to the anachronism of 'just going on strike' by what follows
concerning a 'walk-out' from the state, *divortium*, literally 'divorce'.

G

very desertion would prove your punishment. Doubtless
you would be terrified at your loneliness, at everything
gone silent, at a certain stillness as of a world that is dead.
You would search about, whom you could govern. You
would be left with more enemies than citizens. For at
present you have fewer enemies when seen against the
multitude of the Christians, against the fact of having
almost all the citizens of almost every state Christians.
Humankind has always deserved nought of good from
God's hands. . . . Yet, if we compare calamities of
former times, they fall more lightly now, since God gave
Christians to the world.[49]

Cyprian, Bishop of Carthage, two generations later, is again
a stern eschatological figure—and no wonder. The final
half-century of bitter struggle between the Church and the
pagan Empire has just begun. Cyprian despairs of this
world which 'has now grown old . . . and comes to an
end'. Yet it is from Cyprian there comes a verse of that
hymn, which all Christians of the West use as *the* hymn
for occasions of triumph, *Te Deum*. It was Cyprian who
wrote:

> The glorious company of the Apostles,
> The regiment of the exulting Prophets,
> The numberless throng of Martyrs.[50]

But we may be thankful that another, after the persecutions
were past, added the fourth line:

> The holy Church throughout all the world.[51]

It always has seemed most strange to me that, at this very
time—the eve of persecutions, on an imperial scale and
meant utterly to destroy—Origen should have been able to

[49] *Apology*, 37, 40.
[50] Cyprian, *On Mortality*, 26.
[51] Niceta of Remesiana; see A. E. Burn, *The Hymn Te Deum and its
Author*.

look out upon the world with new definition in his hope, the first to proclaim the possibility of a Christian world:

> Every religion will be overthrown, and that of Christians alone prevail. Yes, it, it alone, will someday prevail, as its doctrine takes possession of minds on an ever greater scale. . . . What if not only, as at present, very few were to be in agreement, but the whole Empire of Rome? . . . He said, ' Be of good cheer; I have overcome the world ', and truly He has. . . . It is not only possible but even literal truth that all, the inhabitants of Asia and of Europe and of Africa, Greeks and barbarians to the world's end, every soul of man should come to agreement under one law.[52]

Then he draws back. And no wonder. For two generations more it was to be a fight to the death:

> Perhaps such a result would indeed be impossible to those who are still in the body, but not to those who are released from it.

But was it not a vision inspired by the Spirit who, our Lord promised, should guide us into all the truth?

[52] *Contra Celsum*, VIII, 68-72.

IV

THE APPROACH TO THE
INTELLECTUAL

Was the wisdom of this world all wrong, and by a Christian to be opposed and discarded? Or was pre-Christian learning itself within the purposes of God, to be claimed by those who rejoiced that God had gone on to full and final revelation of Himself in Jesus Christ? Both attitudes were from the first to be found, and both could claim apostolic precedent. Instead of lingering over this problem, it is my purpose to illustrate, from the greatest representative of the second school of thought, Christianity making its appeal to the educated. We shall discuss, (1) Origen himself; (2) the conversion of a student; (3) the training of a missionary; (4) the answer to the non-Christian mind.

Material for the first section comes from the *Ecclesiastical History* of Eusebius. In dealing with the second and third, we shall be indebted to Gregory, later to be surnamed (nick-named) *Thaumatourgos, '*Wonder-worker'. He was the student; he became the missionary-bishop. It was Origen who converted and trained him. Gregory tells us how, in that essay which he wrote on leaving his master, *Address to Origen* (239). Material for the fourth section is provided by Origen himself, in what is his greatest work, the greatest of all Apologies, until nearly two centuries later there appeared the *De Civitate Dei* of St. Augustine (426), 'Concerning the City of God '. Origen's book is *Contra Celsum*, 'Against Celsus', an anti-Christian writer of some seventy years before. First, then, a glance at Origen himself.

1. *Origen himself:* Origen was born in 185, into a Christian home in Alexandria. His name, ' son of Hor ' (god of the Nile), is a heathen one; but then in the New Testament we have Epaphroditus, whom St. Paul calls 'brother, fellow-worker, fellow-soldier ', and that name ' favoured of Aphrodite ' is not only a goddess', but a none too savoury one's at that! As one has said, ' The martyrs perished because they declined to sacrifice to the gods whose names they bore '. Leonides, the father, was in good circumstances, and sufficiently leisured to undertake the boy's education himself. Eusebius says he could write a book about that education alone, fundamental as it was to all that this child would do, ' notable from his swaddling bands '.[1] Besides all the usual subjects, he grounded him well in knowledge of the scriptures. Then he sent him to complete his education under Clement, second (after Pantaenus) head of that most famous centre of learning of the Early Church.

With such a Christian heritage, when did Origen first consciously claim it as his own? In all Origen's huge output of literature there is hardly anything he tells us about himself. One of the few exceptions is that he says he saw the constancy of the martyrs. Eusebius adds that as a young boy Origen was fired by their example and resolved to follow. The chance was nearly his when he was sixteen. They came at night to arrest his father. Young Origen would have been with him, had not his mother had the presence of mind to hide away his clothes. Strange, how impossible it seemed to go into the street undressed, even when seeking martyrdom! Among all the documents Eusebius found a century and a quarter later, the earliest writing of Origen's was a letter, written at that time to his

[1] *Ecclesiastical History*, VI, 2.

father in prison, saying, 'Mind you do not recant because of us'.

The father died for the Faith. The son was to live for it. The State confiscated the property of the martyr. Origen was faithful to the undertaking implicit in his letter. As eldest of the seven sons, he supported his mother and the family by his earnings as a teacher. At the impossibly early age of eighteen, he became head of the famous school where his education had been completed. He was to give it twenty-seven years, the larger half of his remaining life, and for the rest, continue similar work at Caesarea.

All his life's work was Christian scholarship, and to this he gave himself. He sold the library of manuscripts, which he had inherited and collected, to provide himself with a small annuity, comparable to a couple of shillings a day— the sort of living that any beggar might hope to get from charity. He lived on that, refusing share in students' fees or admirers' patronage, and rejoicing in his academic freedom. He held the ideal of apostolic poverty, for years went barefoot, wore a single garment, slept on the ground. And if he lived hard, he worked hard. He learned Hebrew, an almost unheard of ambition in a Christian then, not only to get at the Old Testament, but at Jewish exposition of it. And then he studied Neo-Platonism, to be at home with all the latest movements in Greek thought. Some of this generation are so busy reaffirming the Hebraic in our religion that they seem inclined to deny any debt to Greece. With Origen, there are few denials. Hebrew and Rabbinics, on the one hand; and on the other Christianity as that which gives meaning to the whole heritage of thought. Philosophy, he says:

is neither at variance to the law of God at all points, nor in harmony with it in all.

But for his part he is going to know all he can about both, and fully to relate the two. He was a literary critic, collating manuscripts and versions, discussing date and authorship and text, all in the most modern fashion. As commentator, Epiphanius says, he covered the whole of scripture. And that (for Epiphanius) is not much of an exaggeration. As a preacher he left masses of sermons. Some of this vast output is because, when he was over sixty, Ambrose, a man of means, who had become his fervent disciple, prevailed upon him to be allowed to supply seven ' tachygraphers '—which is what the ancient world called stenographers, ' quickhand ' (not ' shorthand ') writers. We owe even more to this Ambrose, because it was he who urged the Master to write the long overdue reply to the anti-Christian Celsus.

Much of this teaching, preaching, and writing, was missionary work, because it was meant to touch heathens as well as his Christian following. Two spectacular missionary efforts we should not overlook. When still a young man he was sent for by the mother of the Emperor, Alexander Severus, ' a most pious woman if ever there was one ', says Eusebius. She had heard of his fame, and was interested in enquiring about his religion. She sent a military escort to fetch him, and thus he preached to royalty at Antioch. In later life he heard that the Emperor Philip was at least interested in the Christians (he was said to have gone to church on Easter Eve, and not been offended when they made him sit among the penitents). Eusebius found among extant documents copies of Origen's letters to him and to Severa his Empress. The man who was first to envisage the possibility of a Christian world, was swift to act when there was a chance to bring our religion to the Imperial throne.

In youth he had just missed martyrdom. In old age, in the persecution under the next Emperor, Decius (250-2), he suffered to the verge of death:

He endured for the word of Christ imprisonment and torture, torment under the iron collar and in the dungeon. For several days while his feet were stretched as wide as the stocks would go, they threatened him with the fire, and other things besides, but he bore it patiently.[2]

It shortened his life, and he died at the age of sixty-nine. He had trained hundreds of martyrs. The Church on earth has never beatified him, but who can doubt that he too received the crown of life?

2. *The conversion of a student:* Gregory tells his own story as well as singing the praises of his (as he calls him) 'beloved Head'. He was born into a home of some distinction in the leading city of Pontus, borderland of Roman civilization. A good family—but heathen, and with no likelihood of change, he says, 'under my superstitious father'. When he was fourteen his father died, and from about that time he dates the first visit to him of the *Logos*. He 'thought little of it at the time'—was it some adolescent aspiration towards the Good, like Augustine's when he first read the *Hortensius* of Cicero?—but looking back he sees a guiding hand. His mother had him further educated. She and the family, and Gregory himself, assumed (the local aristocracy would aspire that way) that his future would be in the public service. So he read Latin literature and studied Roman law. And then he planned to go abroad; where was the best place for study? Beirut was nearer but was it so good as Rome? And then there came that mysterious *Logos* again. The Roman Governor of Palestine had Gregory's brother-in-law on his staff. His sister was due to rejoin her husband there. A military escort arrived for her, just as the young brother had packed and was ready for a journey, but had not yet decided where. So he did decide—to go with her to Caesarea, and then on to law studies in Beirut:

Everything pushed me—doing right by my sister, the matter of my own education; what is more, the soldier— I ought to mention this—bringing a permit for more

[2] *Ecclesiastical History*, VI, 39.

public vehicles than were necessary, and travel warrants for us in larger number than my sister alone could account for. These were the surface reasons. Less obvious but truer were—fellowship with this man, education by him in the truth concerning the Word (*Logos*), and the profit of my soul to salvation. It was for these that, blind and ignorant, I was guided hither—for my part, savingly. So then it was not that soldier, but a certain divine Companion, good Guide and Guard, who was leading me safely along . . . till He brought me and settled me here.

It must have been the year 234. He had not thought of staying at Caesarea, but the scholar from Alexandria had moved three years before, and already his fame was great, even in this despised province.

In the year 1945 I was in Palestine, if not with a military escort, with a staff car and an army driver. Driving south on the coast road from Haifa I saw a cart-track and an obscure signpost, 'To Caesarea'. 'Turn right,' I told the surprised driver. I felt a bit surprised myself because the ruts were deeper than I had thought, but there is one thing about ruts—being in, you cannot turn back. And perhaps I shared Gregory's view that 'public vehicles' are there to be used. So on we went. The Roman capital, seat of Pontius Pilate and his successors, is now an obscure Arab village. One can see stones from Roman buildings mixed with the mud-brick of their cottages. Noble columns, long overthrown, now serve as a breakwater. I found the granary of a farm which was clearly the crypt of a Crusader church, and on a higher level among the same farm buildings, one with a rounded apse, as clearly the sanctuary. Did the Crusaders build where there were ruins of an earlier church? For tradition says that the first church-building was on the site of the home of Cornelius. Peter and Cornelius—and one must think too of Paul the prisoner, and Luke; and Philip and the 'four daughters, virgins, which did prophesy ' . . . and, not least, of Origen. And the Arab village became again a place where all the world, and all the world-to-come, were opened up before the eyes of youth. That is the regard for Origen which one catches from Gregory Thaumatourgos. This *Address to Origen* gives an unequalled description of Christian higher education in the third century.

Origen, he says, taught them Logic, Geometry, Physics, Ethics, Literature, Philosophy, and, at a later stage, the Bible, and Christian Doctrine. And this is how there happened something which no words but Gregory's own can describe, for all things that ever happen, this one is a man's own :

> Like some spark it came dropping into my inmost soul. And there, being kindled and catching fire, was love: Love towards the Word (*Logos*) Himself, most alluring to all by reason of beauty unspeakable, the holy, the most lovely. And love towards this man, His friend and representative. By this love sore wounded, I was induced to give up all the aims which I was proposing to myself, for my affairs and education, among other things, even my law-studies of which I was proud; yes, fatherland and family, both relatives in Caesarea and those left behind at home. I had one regard, one passion—theology, and this godlike man, master therein.

He speaks of Origen's taking him on as a student, just as a skilled farmer might take a wild bit of land, untilled, unfertile, sour, arid, stony, and waste. He surveyed him, took the measure of his capacities, and then got to work. The Master might deal with big subjects but his head was not in the clouds. Down here, at the school in Caesarea, he was careful to know each student individually.

Logic he taught as a fundamental discipline of the mind. Gregory vividly describes the beginning of this hard discipline :

He would accost us in the genuine Socratic manner. There were times when, if he saw us to be quite unresponsive, he would trip us up in the argument, as though we were unbroken colts, leaping out of the course, dashing about getting nowhere. Then by a certain persuasion and compulsion, like a bridle in our mouths, his discourse brought us to a halt, quiet before him. At first it was uncomfortable for us, indeed not without pain. But when he had brought us up to standard, made us ready for receiving the words of truth . . . he dealt bountifully with us.

His Geometry he made a real 'ground-work' for knowledge. His Astronomy—taught as a part of Physics—

made the heavens attainable to us, as though by a ladder reaching to the sky.

Gregory's education had been largely Latin and legal. Here he read Greek literature, and Origen was the first to introduce him to Greek Philosophy. And then:

Concerning (the Humanities) he counselled us, 'Do not give yourselves to any of them, though someone be acclaimed as all-wise by all mankind, but only to God and His prophets'. And he himself became interpreter of the prophets, and explained whatever was dark and involved. Because the Author of all men, who stands behind the prophets, beloved of God, and prompts every prophecy and mystic and divine discourse, has honoured this man as friend, and set him as representative. And that of which through others He hints in riddles only, through this man He turns into a full course of instruction. . . .

The greatest gift this man has received from God, this portion wholly good is his from heaven, that he should be interpreter of the words of God to man, himself to explain the things of God as though it were God speaking, and to describe them to men in such a way as they might hear. . . .

And so to us there was nothing that might not be talked of, no knowledge that was hidden or out of reach. . . . We were allowed with all frankness to go the whole round, to make enquiries everywhere, to satisfy ourselves on every subject, and to enjoy things good for the soul. . . . In short, he was a paradise to us, after the likeness of the great Paradise of God.

He ends the address:

Beloved Head,
who didst save us when present at thy holy lessons, save us by thy prayers, even when gone abroad!

3. *The training of a missionary:* As a missionary Gregory is the most brilliant example of so much in the preceding chapters, that if we use familiar subheadings to summarize his work, we shall be illustrating almost all our findings hitherto. How did he preach?

(i) The attack on polytheism: Origen not only prayed for his student after his five years' study were over, and he had gone down. He wrote to him, and urged him to consecrate his gifts to the service of God. In Pontus he, being of their own aristocracy, was regarded as a natural leader. The fact that he did so consecrate himself—and accept consecration as bishop—meant that he was able to lead a whole population into the Christian fold. His see is said to have contained only seventeen Christians then. At his death there remained only seventeen pagans. It is obvious that in such a tradition, whatever its exaggerations, we have something more than individual conversions. Three factors produce this, the first large scale mass movement in Christian history. First, this is the frontier of the Empire, where life is less individualized, and the community is likely to move together under its natural leaders (as we have had to learn in so many mission fields to-day). Second, Gregory

is such a natural leader. Third, he is extraordinarily gifted.
Polytheism is attacked and—disappears. There happens,
first in Pontus, what Origen has already seen (and said)
will happen throughout the Roman world.

(ii) Exorcism: Among his gifts, Gregory had this gift
(*charisma*). Behind the many stories of miracles, some of
them extravagant, which gave to him the name 'Wonder-
worker', we can see a power in him which is recognized as
greater than that of the local gods, able to heal, able to cast
out devils. He once did it unwittingly, stopping for a night
in a temple, while a storm raged outside. In the morning
the heathen priests came to perform their office and nothing
would go right. His presence had robbed the shrine of its
numina. So he wrote on a paper 'Gregory to Satan—you
may come back'—and the priests felt all was well. An idol
festival, turned from joy to mourning by outbreak of a
pestilence, finds him there to heal the multitude. The
pestilence is removed—and so are the idols.

(iii) The life of the Church: Part of his success in dealing
with this mass-movement was that he used his knowledge of
local custom, in arranging for festivals in honour of the
martyrs (after the Decian persecution) to take the place of
pagan feasts. Here I discern again his master, Origen's,
influence. In a letter, Origen urges him to 'spoil the
Egyptians'. He means primarily to tell his student 'Go on
studying the Greek philosophers, in order to equip yourself
for the service of the Christian Church'. But if ancient
pagan learning, why should not contemporary and local
pagan customs be made to contribute to the Church's
growth?

(iv) Use of the scriptures: This adaptation of heathen
customs was a missionary policy not without dangers.
Lurking vestiges of the old polytheism might well make
saints' days something heathen still, far removed from
Biblical religion. Notice then how Origen's letter proceeds:

I tell you from my experience that not many take from

Egypt only the useful, and go away and use it for the service of God. Many produce heretical notions, and set them up like the golden calf.

He ends:

Do you then, my son, diligently apply yourself to the reading of the Holy Bible. Apply yourself, I say.

Origen, the first to foretell the conversion of the Roman Empire, we may well recognize again to be speaking in the spirit of prophecy. The mass-movement conversions which, centuries later, were to sweep our own ancestors into Christendom, failed just here. Much was taken over from pre-Christian religious practices, to speed and ease the conversion of the barbarians. That was not wrong in itself, but Origen's warning was needed. Much that was really pagan did survive. Origen's corrective, a Bible-centred Christianity, was that which was lacking, and which in later centuries others had to struggle to achieve.

A more vivid picture than we have yet seen of an early missionary at work now unfolds. Gregory of Nyssa, who only just missed being a contemporary, thus describes a day in the life of Gregory Thaumatourgos:

At daybreak the crowd would again be at the doors, men, women, and children, those suffering from demon possession, or other afflictions or illnesses of the body. And he in the midst would, in the power of the Spirit, apportion as befitted the need of each of those who had come together. He would preach, he would join an enquiry, he would advise, he would teach, he would heal. It was above all for this that he drew the numbers to the preaching, that sight corresponded with hearing, and that it was through both sight and hearing that the tokens of the divine power shone forth upon him. For his discourse would astonish their hearing, and his wonders among the sick their sight. The mourner used to be cheered, the youth be taught self-control, the aged be tended with fitting words. Slaves were taught to act dutifully towards masters, those in authority to be kind to men under them, the poor that virtue is the one wealth, the property which all are in a position to have a chance at. The rich man was urged to have a care for others, and that he was the steward of possessions rather than the owner of them.

4. *The answer to the non-Christian mind:* If that is a worthy *sight* of early missionary preaching, this book shall end with a worthy *sound* of the same.

Celsus' book was called *Alethes Logos,* best translated 'True Religion'. It was the most formidable attack on Christianity yet made, one of the most formidable ever. He campaigns against what he believes to be superstition and fanaticism; above all against a religion which divides men from their fellows and is thus dangerous to society and the state. Many of his objections sound familiarly modern. There are intellectuals of our own time of whom they may remind us. For some have not only found the Christian way impossible to accept themselves, but have used their pens, like Celsus, in anti-Christian attack. As, reading the following pages, one seems to hear the argument proceeding, the centuries will fall away, and it might well be these moderns making their controversial case. It is good that we should feel this relevance, but let us add to it one thought more. However up-to-date Celsus' objections may appear, they are after all eighteen centuries old. That thought denies the unbeliever's assumption that his position is the latest product of the modern scientific outlook. What is more, it is only in Origen's *Contra Celsum* that these paragraphs of Celsus exist. The anti-Christian objections we should never have heard of but for their inclusion in the more than adequate reply. It is not true that the best minds have belonged to the pagans.

The translation which follows is from the first two of the eight books of the *Contra Celsum.* One more or less connecting argument seemed to be the only way to sample so immense a work. I have had to telescope passages into each other, abbreviate all the way, and omit more than I have included. Yet there is far more of direct translation than of paraphrase, and I trust that I have nowhere misrepresented Origen's meaning nor inserted any of my own. For brevity's sake I have set down under the respective names, 'Celsus', 'Origen', the objection and the reply, and occasionally, where a gap could not otherwise be bridged, inserted a few sentences of explanation.

A list of the subjects dealt with will show that difficulties to the non-Christian mind of the second century are not far removed from the twentieth. For what Celsus and Origen here discuss are:

> Rationalism,
> The Virgin Birth,
> The reality of Religious Experience,
> Was Jesus divine?
> Miracles,
> The Resurrection Appearances.

ORIGEN: When our Saviour and Lord, Jesus Christ, was faced with false-witnesses, He said nothing. Denounced, He answered not a word. He believed that His whole life and His deeds among the Jews were stronger than any voice refuting false witness, or than speech defending against denunciations.

So you see, my good Ambrose, with regard to Celsus' false-witness against Christians in writings, and denunciations in his book, I do not know why you should wish us to make any defence. As if there were not plain refutation in the *facts*. . . . Jesus is always being faced with false-witness. All the time He is being denounced. And now also His way is to say nothing and make no answer with His voice. His defence is in the lives of His true disciples.

And yet, in the multitudes of those who are counted believers some might be found of the sort to be shaken and overthrown by these writings of Celsus, but who would be put right if a defence were made against them. So we have thought it good to be persuaded, and to reply to the book you sent us. Not that I think anyone who has done even a short course in Theology will allow it to be what Celsus entitles it, 'True Religion'!

Let us then hear what Celsus has to say:

CELSUS: It is by use of Reason, and a rational guide, that a man should arrive at the doctrines which he receives. He who assents to opinions otherwise lays himself open to all manner of deceptions. Examples of believing without reason are the begging priests of Cybele, soothsayers, devotees of Mithras and Bacchus, and the like. . . . And so it is with the Christians. . . . Some there are who will neither give nor receive a reason for what they believe. 'Do not examine,' they say, 'only believe.' And, 'Your faith will save you'. And they say, 'Evil is the wisdom of this life, but foolishness is a good thing'.

ORIGEN: The answer to this is that if life were such that all men might retire from business and devote themselves to Theology, no one should follow any other way. For in Christianity you will find, to put it mildly, quite as much critical examination as elsewhere, attempts to explain hard sayings in the prophets, to explain the parables in the Gospels, to explain many more happenings and commands that have symbolic meaning. But for most men that is impossible—they have to earn their living. Many would be incapable. So it is only a few who go after Reason. What better means could have been found for helping the majority than that which was handed down by Jesus for the nations? And ask yourself concerning the multitude of believers, who have been cleared of the mess of sin in which they formerly wallowed—is it better for them to believe without reason, and have their character somehow set right, or should they have said, 'No, we must not allow ourselves to be converted by simple faith. We must wait until we have time to go into all the reasons'—and remained in most sinful life? . . . No good happens among men without God. This is true of the man who has healed folks' bodies and led them to better health. And how much more of Him who has healed souls, converted them, made them better, and brought them to depend on God who is over all. . . ?

Besides, faith without reason is everywhere. Who puts to sea, or gets married, becomes a father, or sows seed in the ground, but in faith that better things will result—though the opposite may, and sometimes does, happen? . . . That which keeps men going, in every undertaking where the outcome is unsure, is hope and faith in a better future. How should not this be so—and *reasonably*—for him whose belief goes beyond the sailed seas, the sown land, the married woman, and the whole gamut of human affairs, to God who created all these things, and to Him who with surpassing comprehension and divine understanding ventured to bring this Gospel to men everywhere in the world, at the cost of great hazard, and a death deemed shameful, which He endured for men's sake; and He taught those who in the beginning were persuaded to the service of His teaching, at the cost of every hazard and with death always at hand, to venture forth everywhere in the world for men's salvation.

[To voice some of his difficulties Celsus puts forward a Jew. Not that there is anything particularly Jewish about the difficulties. But if, as he knows is the case, Christianity takes its rise in Hebrew religion, a Hebrew criticism here may penetrate to the foundations. The Jew is not a convincing figure—one feels all the time that Celsus is doing a ventriloquist's trick. The words come from the Jew, but the thought is that of Celsus. He speaks as if directly challenging Jesus Himself.]

THE JEW: How did you get the notion of birth from a virgin? You were born in a Jewish village of a woman who was poor, a peasant, at her spinning wheel. And he who had taken her to wife, a carpenter by trade, when she was convicted of adultery, put her out. And so, cast out by her husband, she wandered about, and shamefully and in secret she bore this Jesus. And he, because of poverty, went as a hired labourer to Egypt. There he tried his hand at certain powers for which Egyptians are in high repute. Then he returned, and, priding himself on these powers, he used them to proclaim himself a god!

ORIGEN: What Celsus and his Jew say about the Mother of Jesus is significant. They could have falsified the narrative in a different way, and turned it into just an ordinary parentage. But what they do say makes, as it were, an involuntary admission that there *was* something extraordinary about the birth of Jesus. Of course those who would not accept His miraculous birth made up some falsehood—and a simple one would have sufficed. But no! The very form of their falsehood takes account of the fact that it was not by Joseph that the Virgin conceived Jesus.

About this humble origin we will take Celsus and his Jew at their word. Here is our Jesus, reproached with having been born in a village—and that not a Greek one!—among all the nations, belonging to one of no eminence; despised as son of a poor working woman; for His poverty leaving His homeland and going for hire to Egypt. *And He has been able to shake the whole world of men,* beyond not only Themistocles the Athenian, but even Pythagoras and Plato, or any other wise man anywhere in the world, or any king or general. Now, would not anyone who incidentally discovered the nature of these facts be struck with amazement at the triumph of this Man?

THE JEW: When you were bathing in the Jordan, you say that something that had the appearance of a dove dropped down from the sky upon you. Who in the way of a trustworthy witness saw this apparition? Or who heard a voice from heaven adopting you as a son of God—is it only what you yourself say, and evidence which calls in someone of those who are fellow-culprits with you?

ORIGEN: Before we begin to answer, this must be said:
With regard to nearly all history, however true, if you wish
to establish that it did take place, and give an impression
of it that can be retained, this is one of the hardest tasks—in
some cases impossible.   For suppose someone says, 'There
never was a Trojan War, because there are interwoven with
the record some impossible stories '—I do not know how we
should prove it. . . . But he who deals candidly with
history and wishes to keep himself undeceived among it,
judges to which items he will assent, which he will (after
finding out what the authors meant) explain as allegory,
and which he will just disbelieve as written for someone or
other's gratification.   And starting from this, here is what
we have to say about the whole history concerning Jesus
in the Gospels: We do not invite acute minds to a simple
and unreasoning faith.   We would show that there is need
for candour in those who deal with them, and of much
critical examination, and, so to speak, of getting at the purpose of the writers, so that it may be discovered with what
intention everything was written. . . .

To draw parallels to this particular record, I would say
to the Jew, even your own Ezekiel wrote saying, 'The
heavens were opened and I saw visions of God ', and Isaiah
wrote, 'I saw the Lord of hosts sitting upon a throne, high
and lifted up '. How do we know if he really saw it? . . .
And which of them is more worthy of belief when he says
the heavens were opened to him and he heard a voice . . .
Isaiah, Ezekiel, or Jesus?   For of these two there is no
achievement to be found anything like so great.   But the
good works of Jesus do not belong just to the time when
He was here in the flesh.   Right up to the present His
power is producing conversion and a changed life in those
who believe in God through Him.   And a clear proof that
these things are done by His power is that, although as He
Himself said there are not labourers to labour in the harvest
of souls, the harvest *is* so great of those who are gathered
and brought in to those threshing floors of God—found

everywhere—I mean the churches. There are still traces, you see, preserved among Christians, of that Holy Spirit once seen in the form of a dove.

With regard to *that* appearance, I do not myself take it that the visible heaven was opened and its structure divided. Perhaps such an admission might be an offence to the more simple-minded, who because of their simplicity set the universe in motion and split up the vast compounded structure of the whole heaven! But he who examines such an incident more profoundly will say that there is, as the Bible puts it, a certain *perception* belonging to the divine, which the blessed alone have come to know already.

CELSUS: The ancient myths ascribed divine origin to Amphion, and Aeacus, and Minos, and—to make this seem less improbable—showed great works and wonders of theirs, truly superhuman. What about Jesus? What good or wonderful thing has He done, in work or word? He showed us no sign, and this though they challenged Him in the Temple to afford clear proof that He was the Son of God.

ORIGEN: Let the Greeks show us, of those instanced, who does anything vital or splendid, which both extends to later generations, and is an achievement such as to give probability to the myths about his being of divine origin. They have nothing to show, which can be put into the same category as what Jesus offers. For we declare that the work of Jesus fills the whole world of men. Throughout the world are the churches of God, founded by Jesus, and made up of those who have been turned from countless sins. And even yet does the name of Jesus take away mental disturbance from men, and cast out devils and diseases, and make a certain wondrous meekness, steadiness of character, love to mankind, goodness and gentleness, in those who—not in pretence for the sake of a living or the supply of any human wants, but genuinely, have accepted the doctrine concerning God and Christ, and the judgment to come.

CELSUS: Supposing we grant that what is written may

be true—about healing, raising the dead, a few loaves feeding a great multitude with many fragments left over, and so much else that his wonder-struck disciples have recorded. There is nothing very extraordinary about this. Look at the tricks of conjurors—promising the while things still more wonderful! Look at the contrivances of those who have learned from the Egyptians! In the middle of the market-place, show them a few coppers and they will show *you* their venerated arts! They will cast devils out of men. They will breathe on their diseases. They will call up the souls of dead heroes. They will display costly banquets and tables and dainties and meats—which are not there! They will set in motion as if alive things which are not really living but do seem like it! Since these folk do so, have we to suppose them to be the sons of God? Or is it to be said that these are the artifices of wicked men and demon-possessed?

ORIGEN: Mark this! He speaks as if accepting the existence of magic. I do not know whether he is the same Celsus as the one who wrote several books against it. It is convenient to him, in what he is out for, to compare with works of magic the miracles recorded of Jesus. And they might have been comparable, if (as is the case with the magicians) it were a matter of showmanship and of His show being better than theirs. But tell me, does any of the conjurors call upon the spectators because of his tricks to reform their characters? Does he take those who are amazed at the sights and train them in the fear of God? Does he try to persuade bystanders so to live as men who have been set right by God? Conjurors do none of these things. They have neither the power, the will, nor the desire to make the setting right of mankind their business. What is more, their own lives are full of the most shameful and scandalous sins. Jesus does it all. He shows the pattern of His noblest life to His disciples so as to urge them on to teach men of God's will; to the rest that, having learned how they ought to live, not so much by His miracles as by His word and

His life, they might do all things with reference to pleasing God above. Compare such a life with the trade of the conjuror? No, surely it is more reasonable to believe that, according to the promise, He is God revealed in human form for the good of our race. And I would add this: Jesus promised that His disciples should do even greater works than those which He showed; this too has been fulfilled. For always there are being opened the eyes of those who were blind in soul. The ears of those who were deaf to words of virtue hear eagerly of God and of the blessed life with Him. Many too who were lame in the feet of the inner man, as the Bible calls it, now healed by the Word, do not simply leap, but leap as the hart—which (let me point out) is an animal hostile to serpents and stronger than all the poison of vipers. And these lame who have been healed, receive from Jesus power to trample, with the very feet formerly lame, upon serpents and scorpions of sin, and in general upon all the power of the enemy.

CELSUS: Did anyone really dead ever rise again with an actual body? Or do you imagine that accounts of others are—as they seem—only myths, while to you there stands discovered a fitting and convincing turning point in your drama—his voice from the cross as he breathed his last, the earthquake, the darkness? So that while still alive, he could not help himself, but once dead he rose again, and showed the marks of his punishment, and the nailprints in his hands. Come, come! Who saw this? A neurotic woman, as you admit. If any other, then one of those mixed up in the same trickery, who according to his state of mind had a dream, or by wishful thinking—this often happens—let his wandering fancy imagine it; or—more likely still—one of them wished to astonish the rest with this wonder, and by such a fraud give a chance to imposters like himself.

ORIGEN: There is one difference from your heroes of Greek mythology. Jesus really died, died a conspicuous death on the cross, so that none might have ground for saying, ' Ah! He purposely withdrew from men's sight, seemed to die—

but did not really—and then appearing again, He did this conjuring trick of rising from the dead!' To me the sure and certain argument is to be found with His disciples, who gave themselves up to a work of teaching full of mortal danger. If they had made up the awakening of Jesus from the dead, could they have taught it so vigorously? Would they at the same time not only have made others prepared to despise death, but themselves have been pre-eminent in doing this very thing?

CELSUS: The fact remains, only those saw him who wanted to. If Jesus wished to show that his power was really divine, he ought to have appeared to those who had reviled him, to him who condemned him, and to people generally.

ORIGEN: This is a formidable attack. It does seem, we agree, according to the Gospels, that after the Resurrection He was not seen as He was before, publicly, and by all. But let us begin with His lifetime. There was only one Jesus—but there were many notions concerning Him, and those who saw Him did not all see the same. Even then He appeared according to the receptivity of the beholder. All men were capable of seeing Him, but they saw differently. After His resurrection from the dead it was a merciful dispensation that some could not see Him at all. Why, even to the Apostles He was not always there, not always manifest, for they could not continuously have received His divinity. After the Resurrection Jesus *had* to be seen, not by all, but by those whom He knew had received eyes capable of seeing His Resurrection. He was sent not only to become known but also to remain hid. For not all that He was was known to those who knew Him—something of Him was hidden even from them; and some there were to whom He was not known at all. And He opened the gates of light to those who were sons of darkness and of night, and who had given themselves to becoming sons of day and of light. And the Lord came as Saviour, like a good Physician, to us who were full of sins, and not to the righteous.

And so we shall go on believing—in God according to the teaching of Jesus Christ, seeking to convert those blind on the subject of religion. Blind, they say, are we; but they themselves are blind. Seducers we, they say; but they lead men astray. Oh, what a noble seduction ours, that men should change from dissolute to sober living—or towards it; to justice from injustice—or tending that way; to wisdom from being foolish—or becoming such; and from cowardice, meanness and timidity, show courage and fortitude, not least in this struggle for the sake of our religion—for God the Creator of all things, and Jesus Christ even as all the prophets have spoken.

DOCUMENTS QUOTED

(Arranged alphabetically, under author's name when authorship is known)

SUGGESTIONS FOR FURTHER READING

THE READER who wishes to turn up passages quoted in this book and to see them in their wider context, will, for all the differences of the older translation, recognize them in the volumes of the Ante-Nicene Christian Library, obtainable in any good library. Eusebius, so often mentioned in the foregoing pages, both for his *Ecclesiastical History* itself, and for his inclusion within it of passages from Apologists and other writers otherwise unknown, may be found in the Library of Nicene and Post-Nicene Fathers. This volume has adequate introduction and notes.

For further knowledge of the life and work of characters mentioned, Smith and Wace, *The Dictionary of Christian Biography* (4 volumes), is invaluable. Harnack's great work, *The Expansion of Christianity* (2 volumes), merits more than most books in this transitory world the appraisal 'of permanent worth'. It will open up many more fields of enquiry than those which this book has sought to enter.

The relevant parts of A. D. Nock, *Conversion: The old and the new in religion from Alexander the Great to Augustine of Hippo*, may with profit be consulted. T. R. Glover's *The Conflict of Religions in the Early Roman Empire*, is a valuable popular treatment of a subject more recently approached, and with weighty scholarship, in C. N. Cochrane's *Christianity and Classical Culture*.

Teachers especially may like to know of a set of six film-strips which the author is preparing on the subject, *The Spread of Christianity*. The first, available from educational suppliers, is called *The Winning of the Roman Empire*, A.D. 29-500. Teachers' notes are issued with it.

INDEX